5×7

5×7 is seven sets of five photographs.

Published by Imaginary Dynamics
imaginarydynamics.com
ISBN: 978-1-971080-00-0

First Edition
File version 1 9 Z 362

There are no disclaimers, warranties, safety notices,
captions, or guarantees for this book or for anything in life.

5×7

Otto Kitsinger

One Fourth

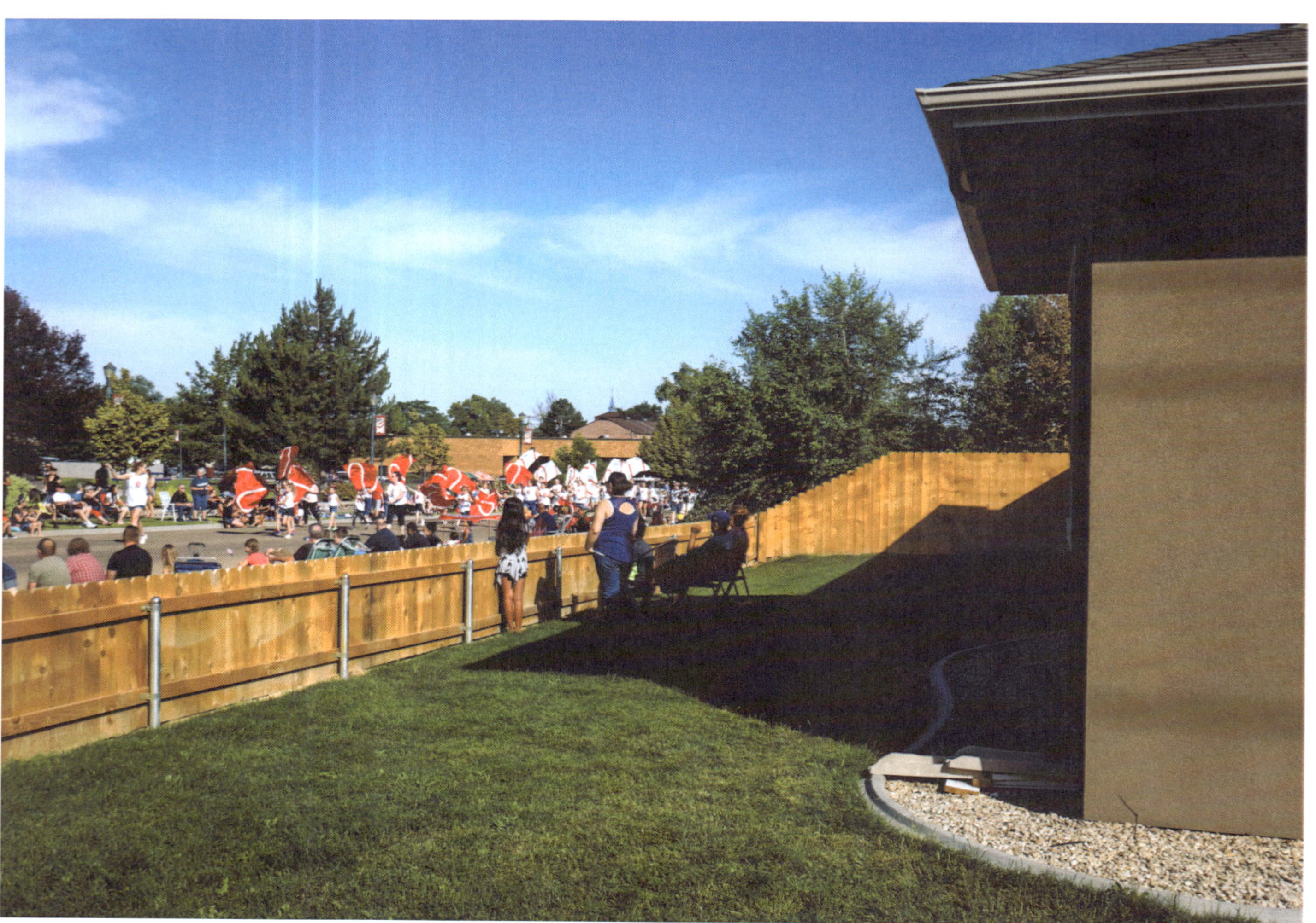

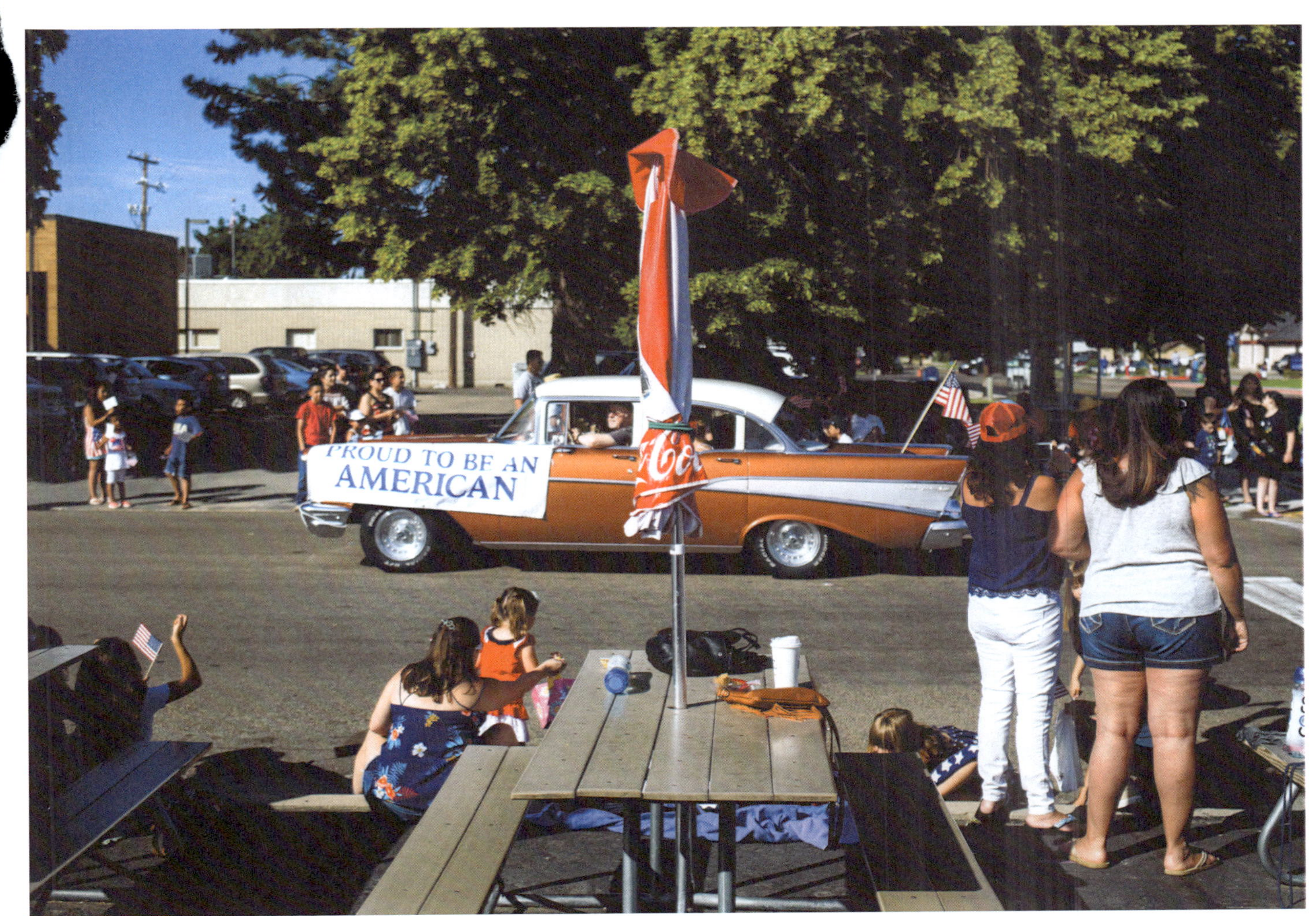

PROUD TO BE AN
AMERICAN

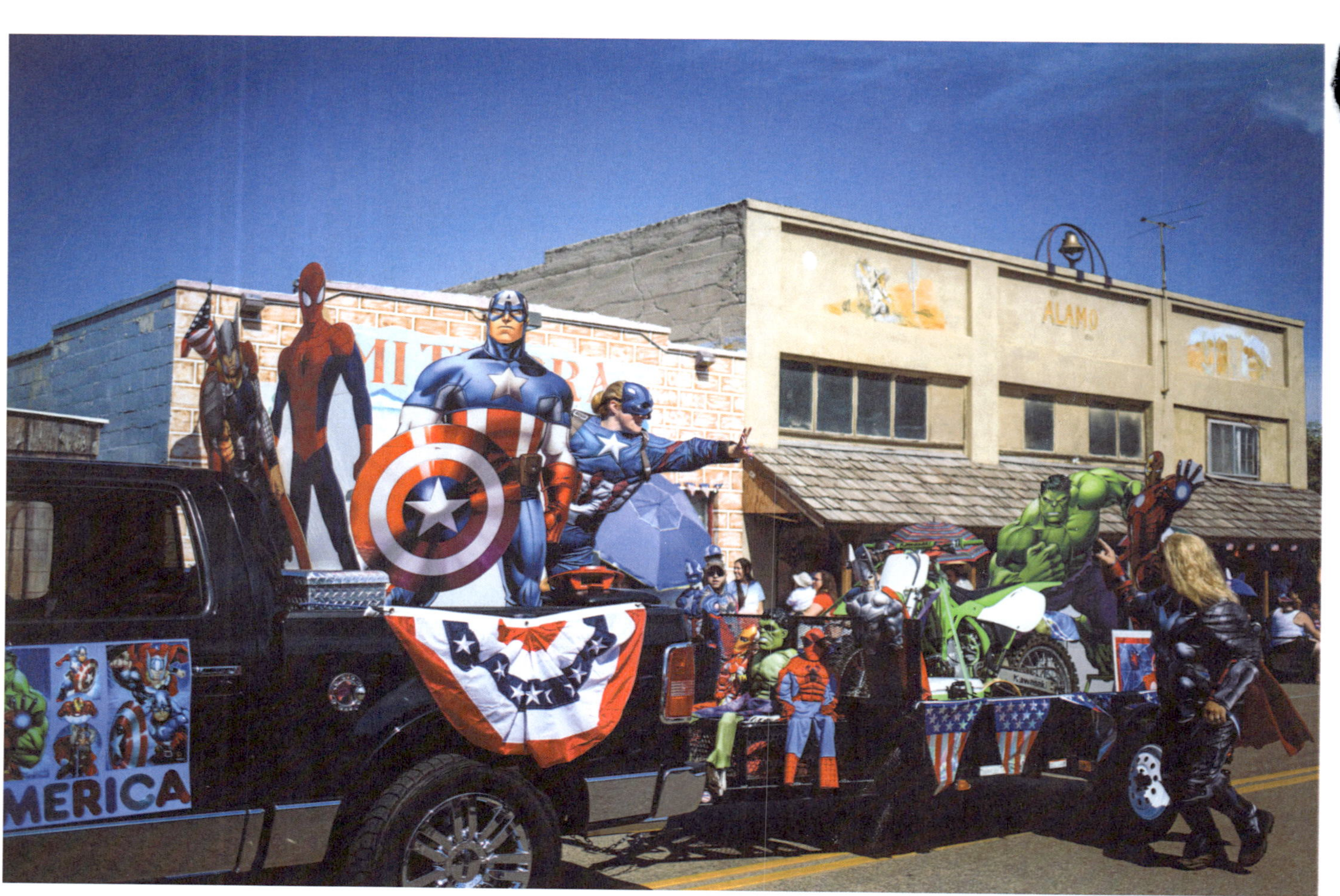

ALAMO
MERICA

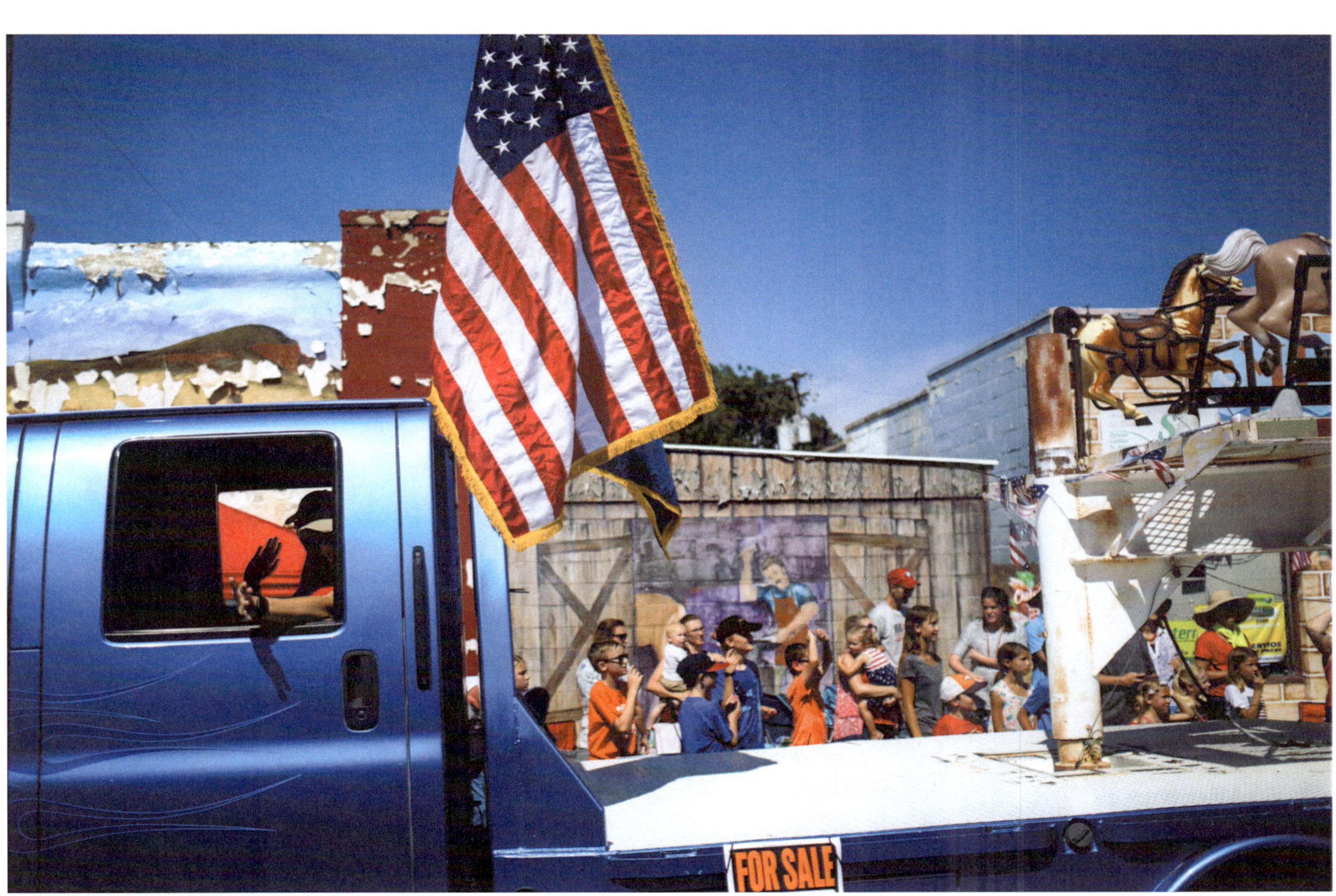
FOR SALE

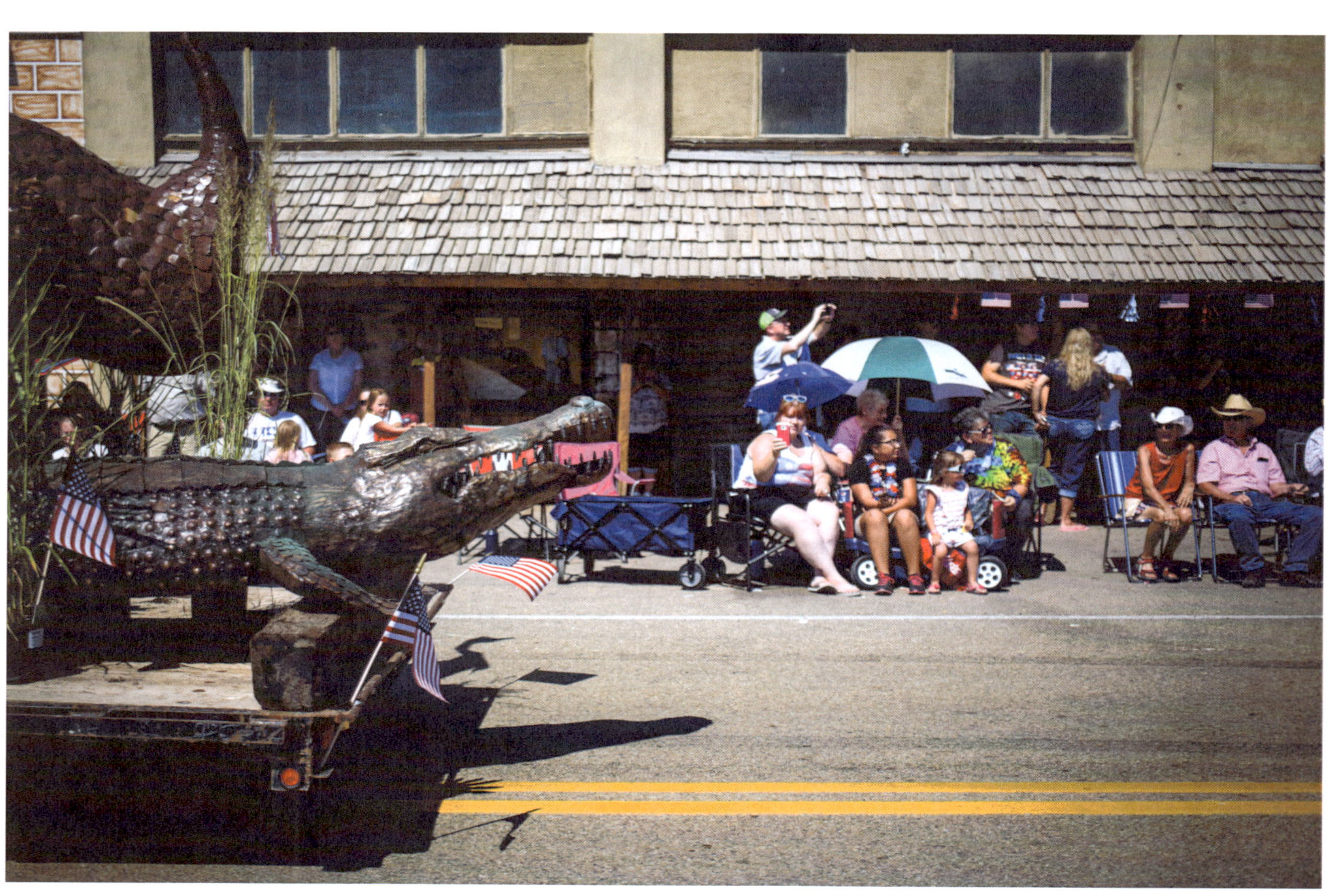

Select guardrails
during 7 hours
5 minutes
and 58 seconds
of May 16th

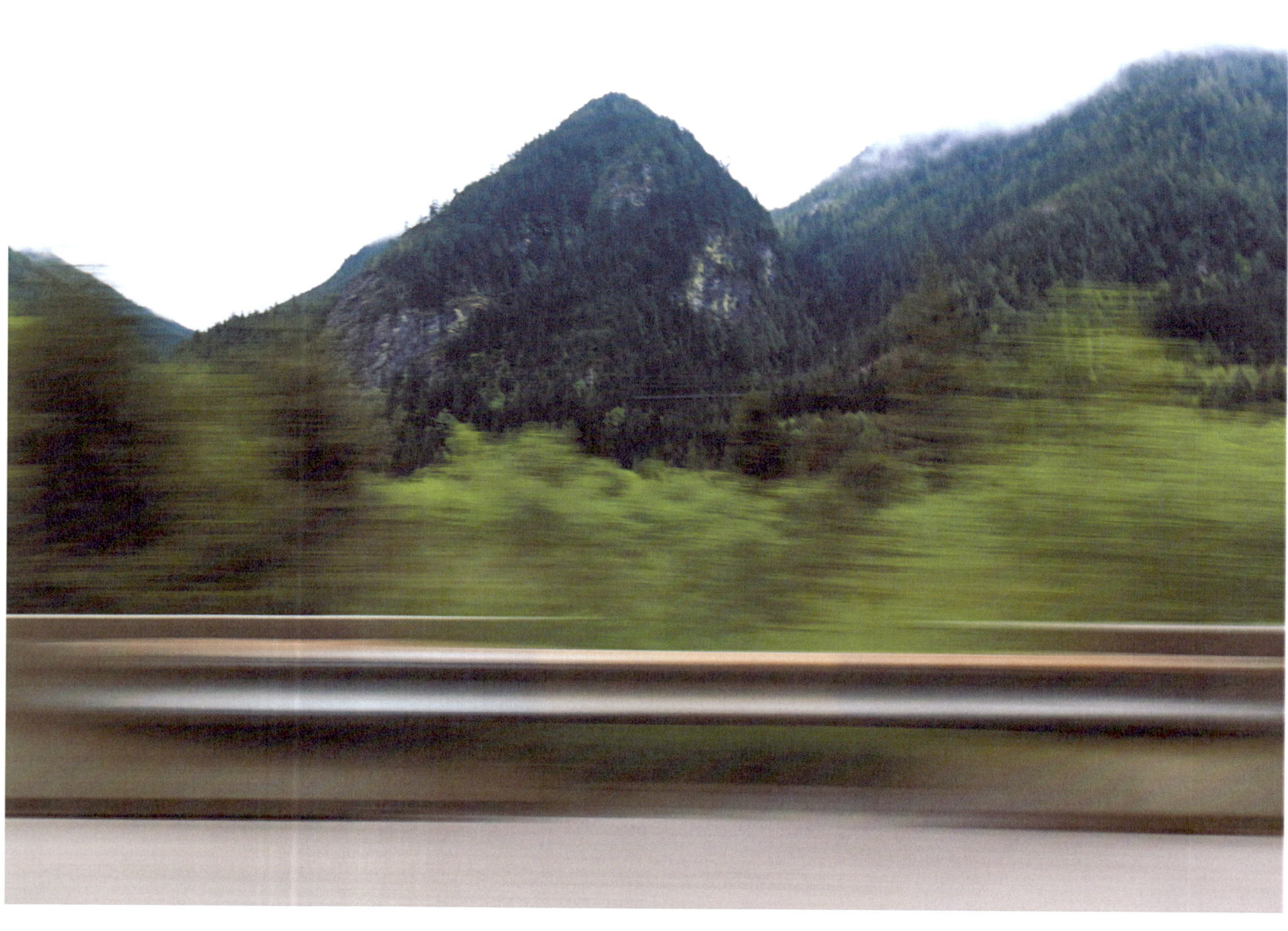

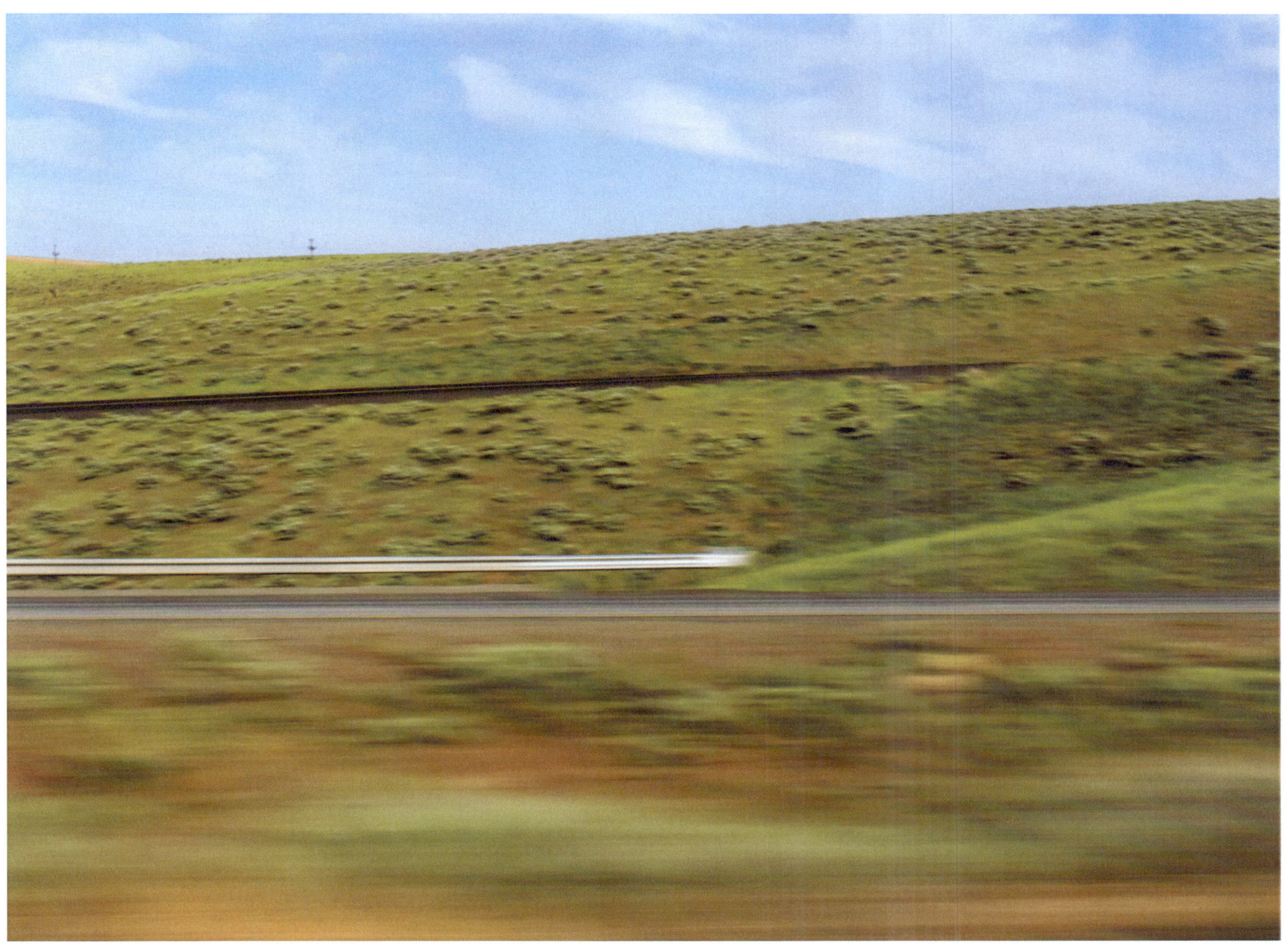

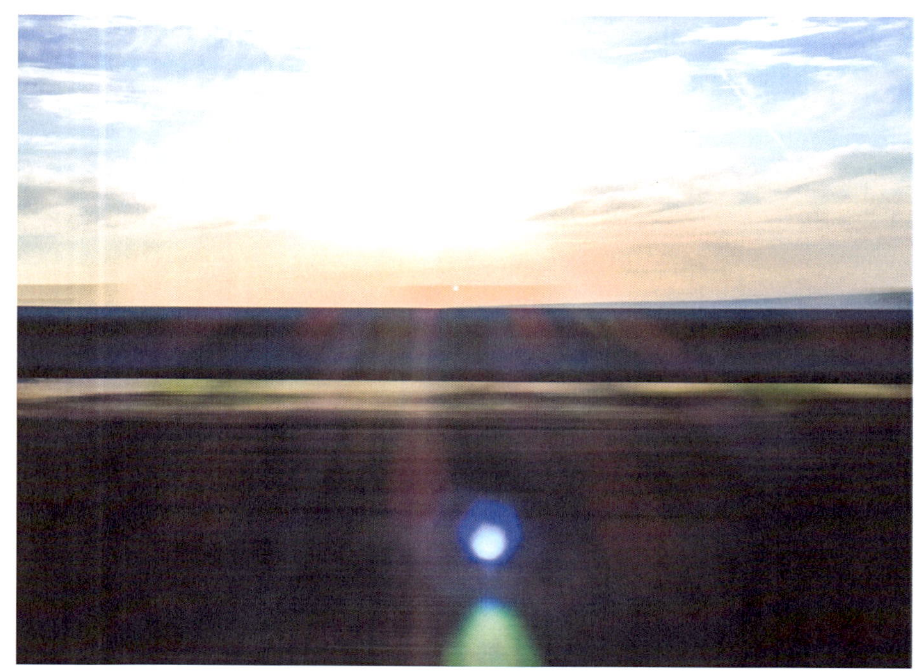

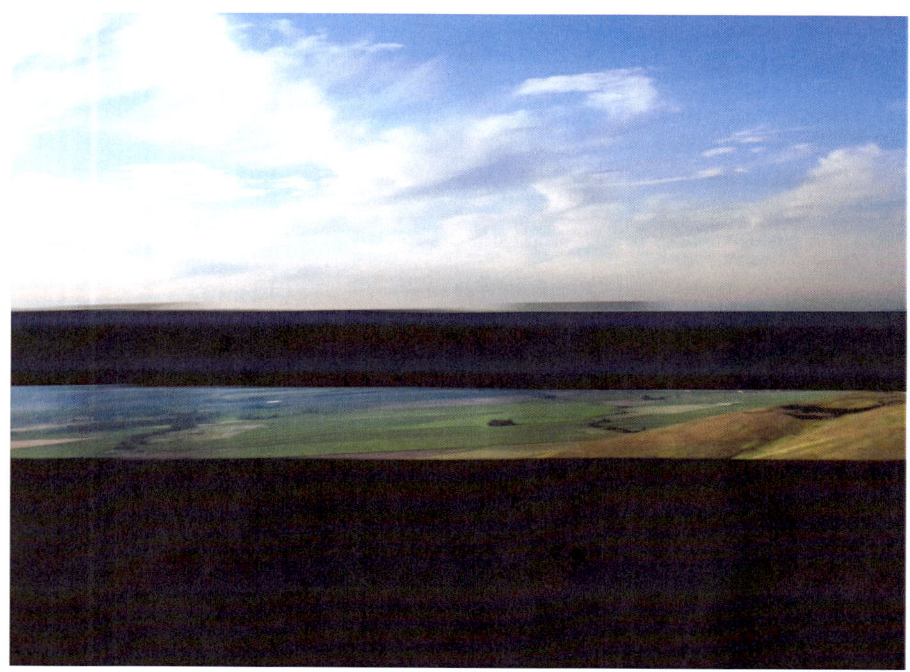

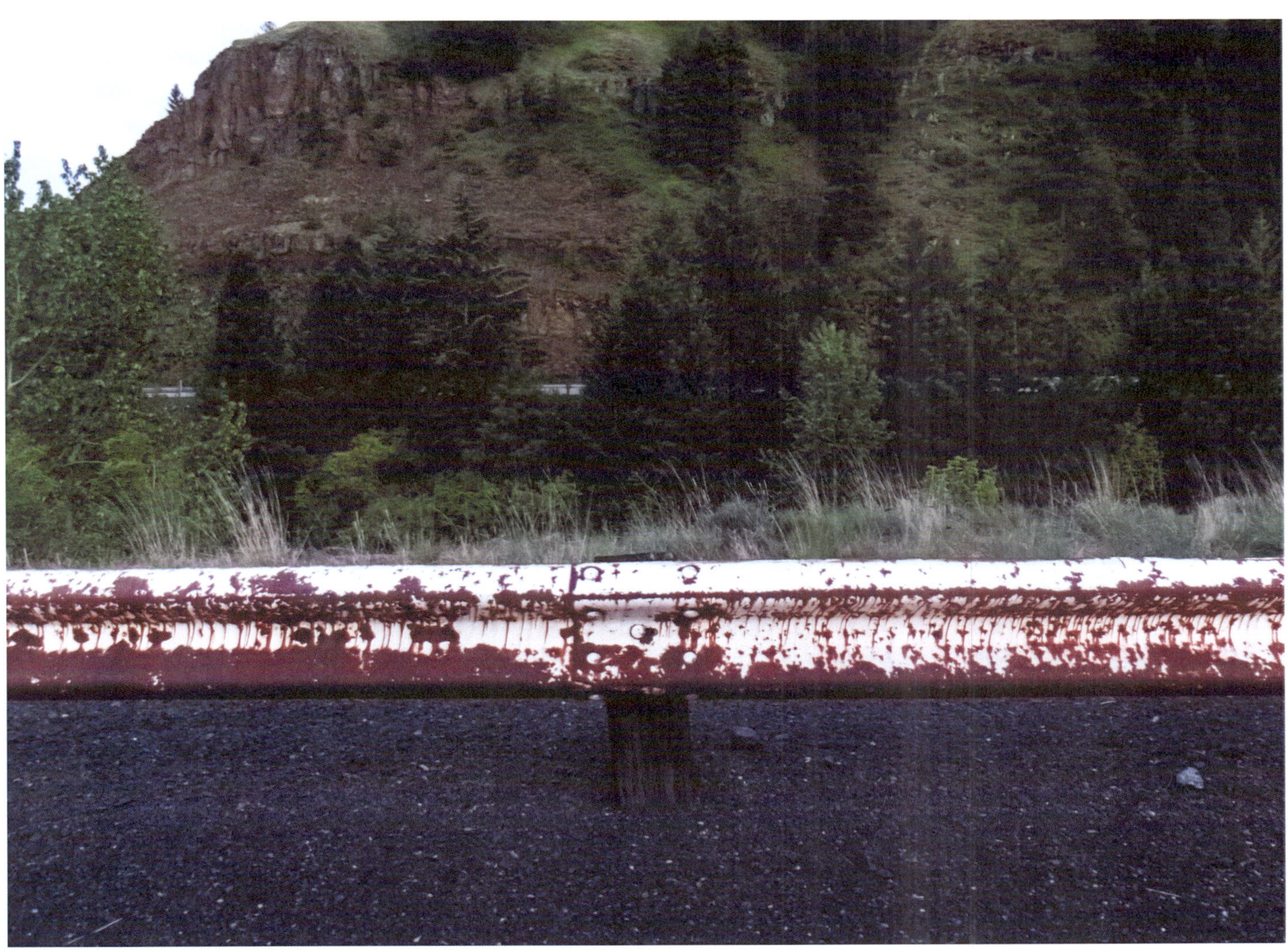

Select picnic tables
of the northbound I-5
Custer, Washington
Rest Area

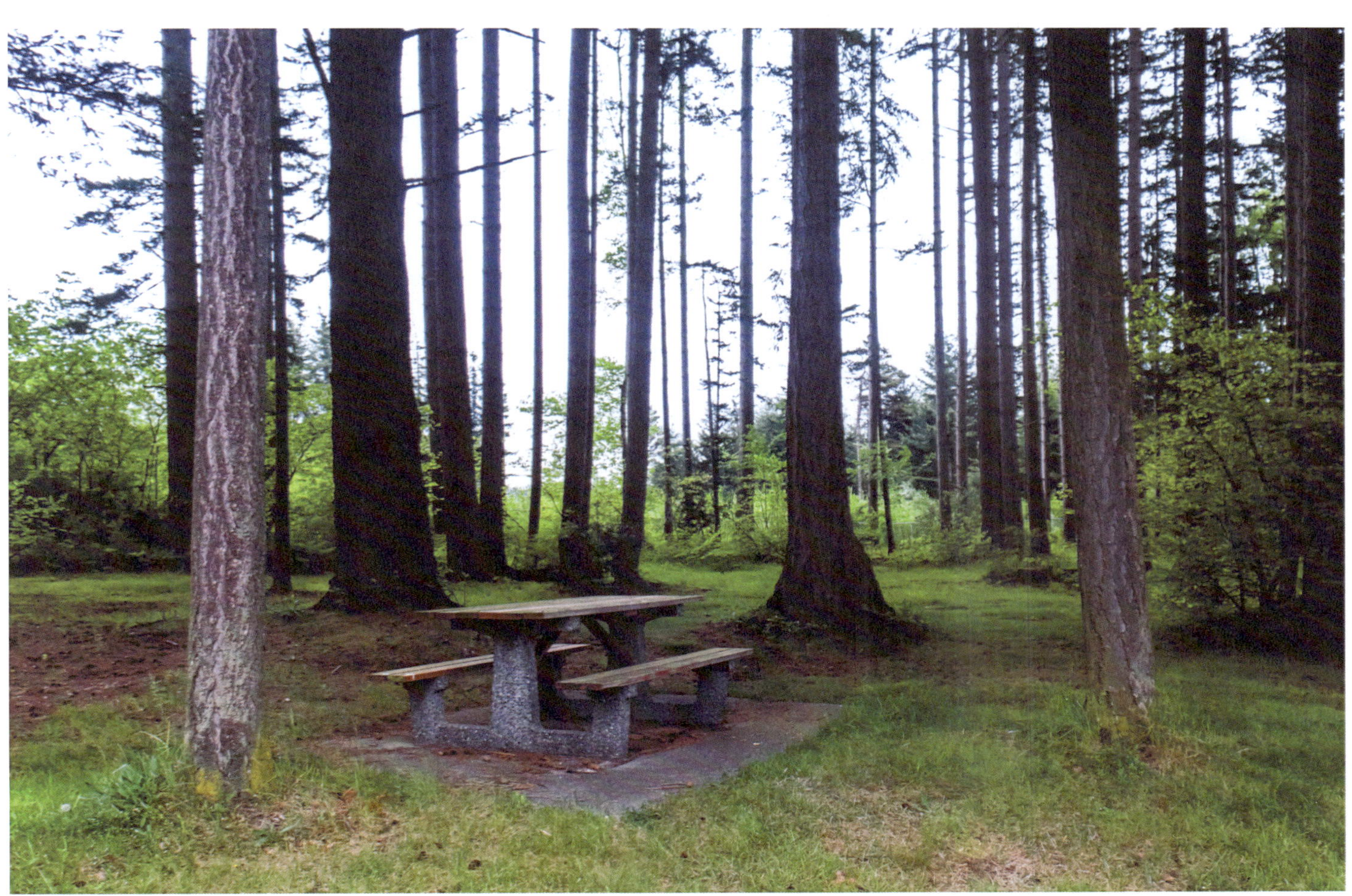

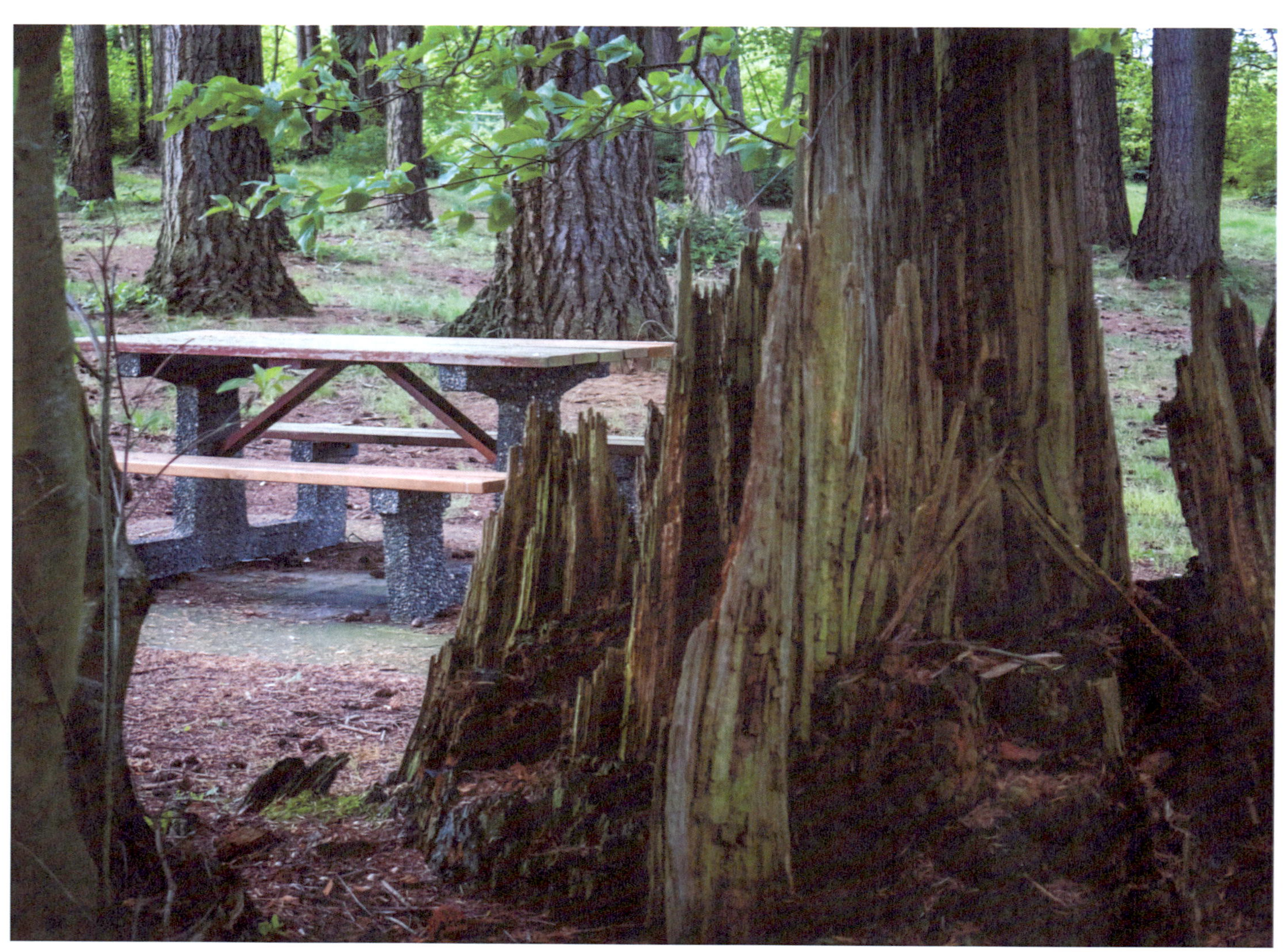

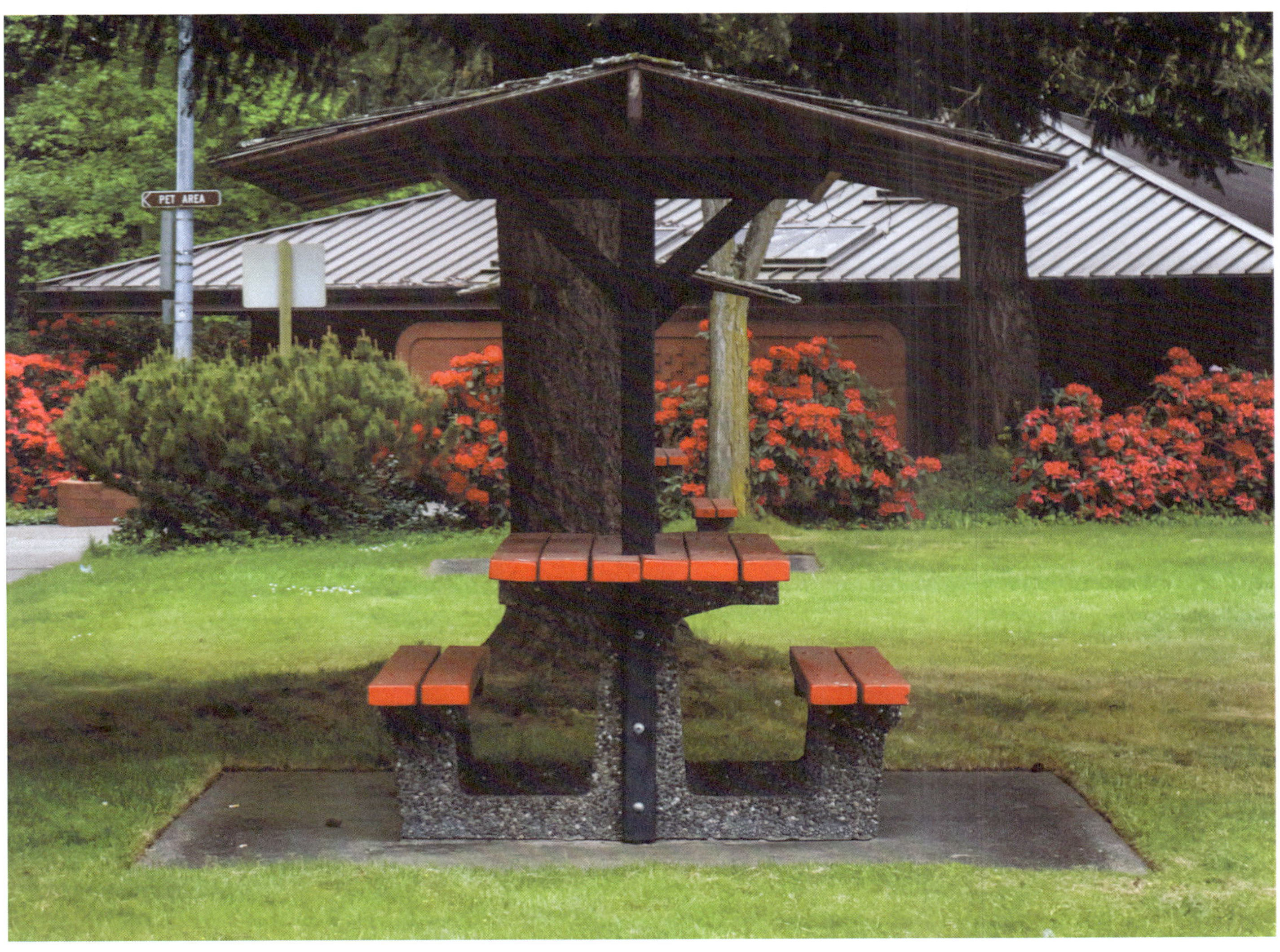
PET AREA

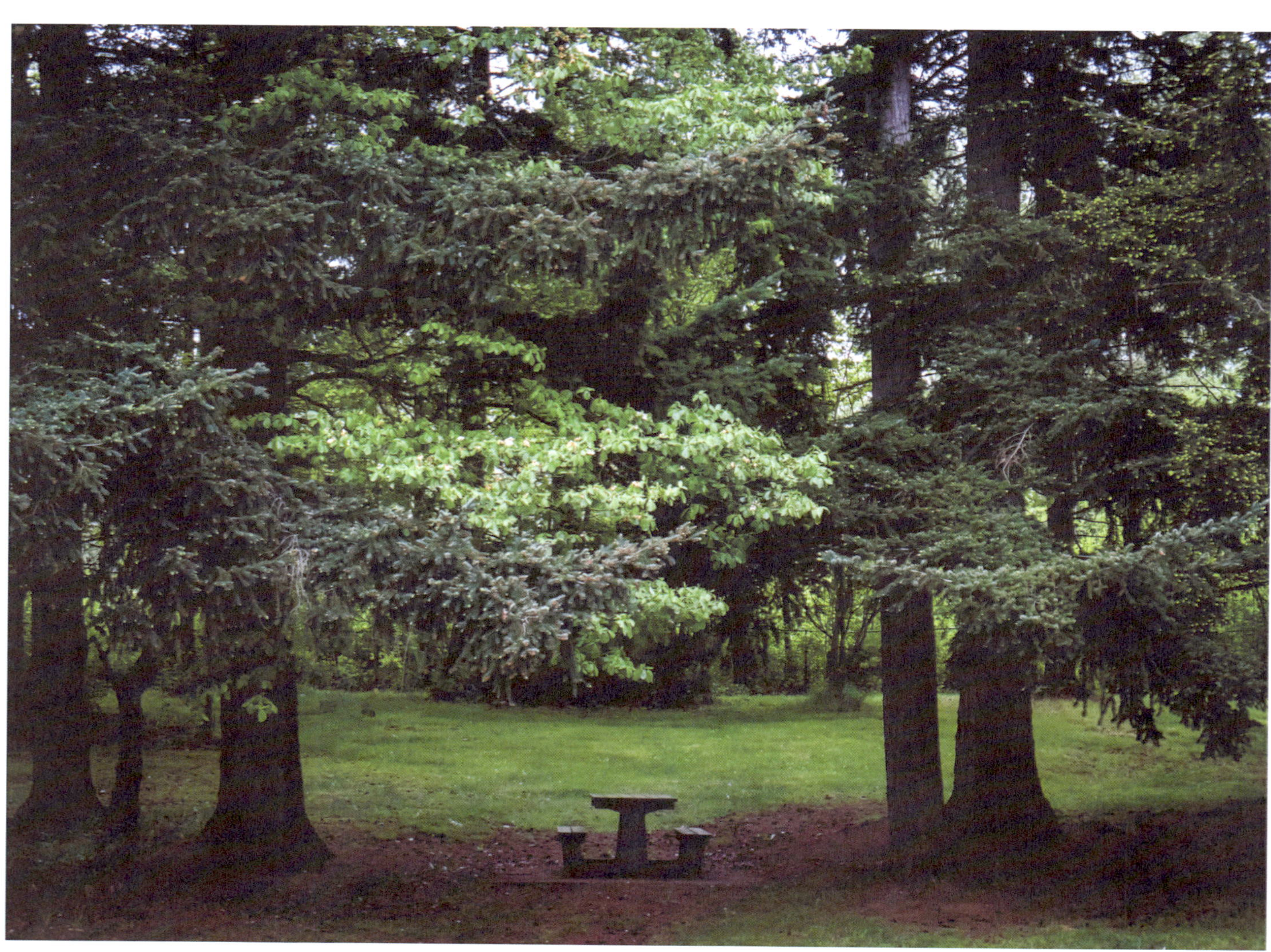

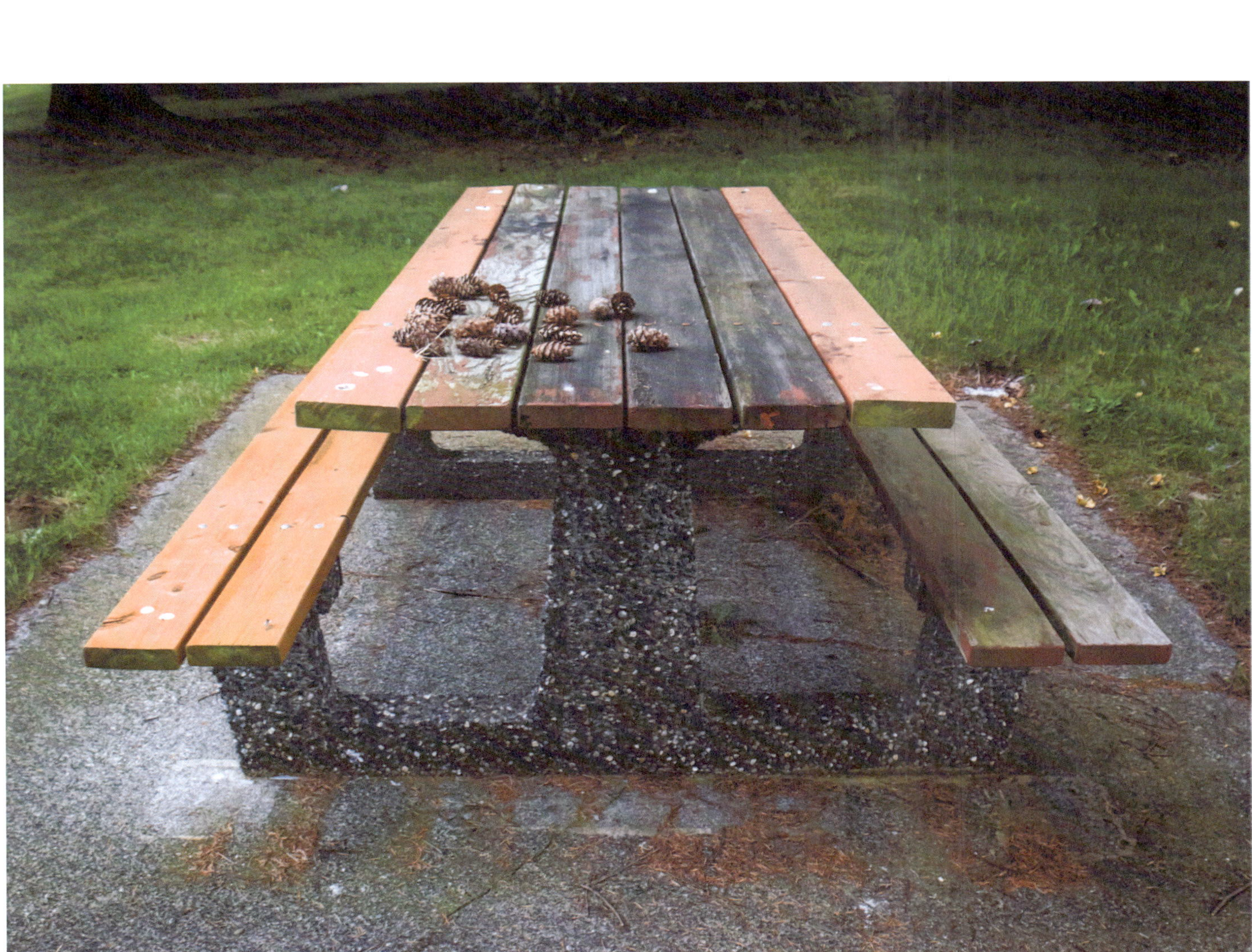

Avoid the crowds

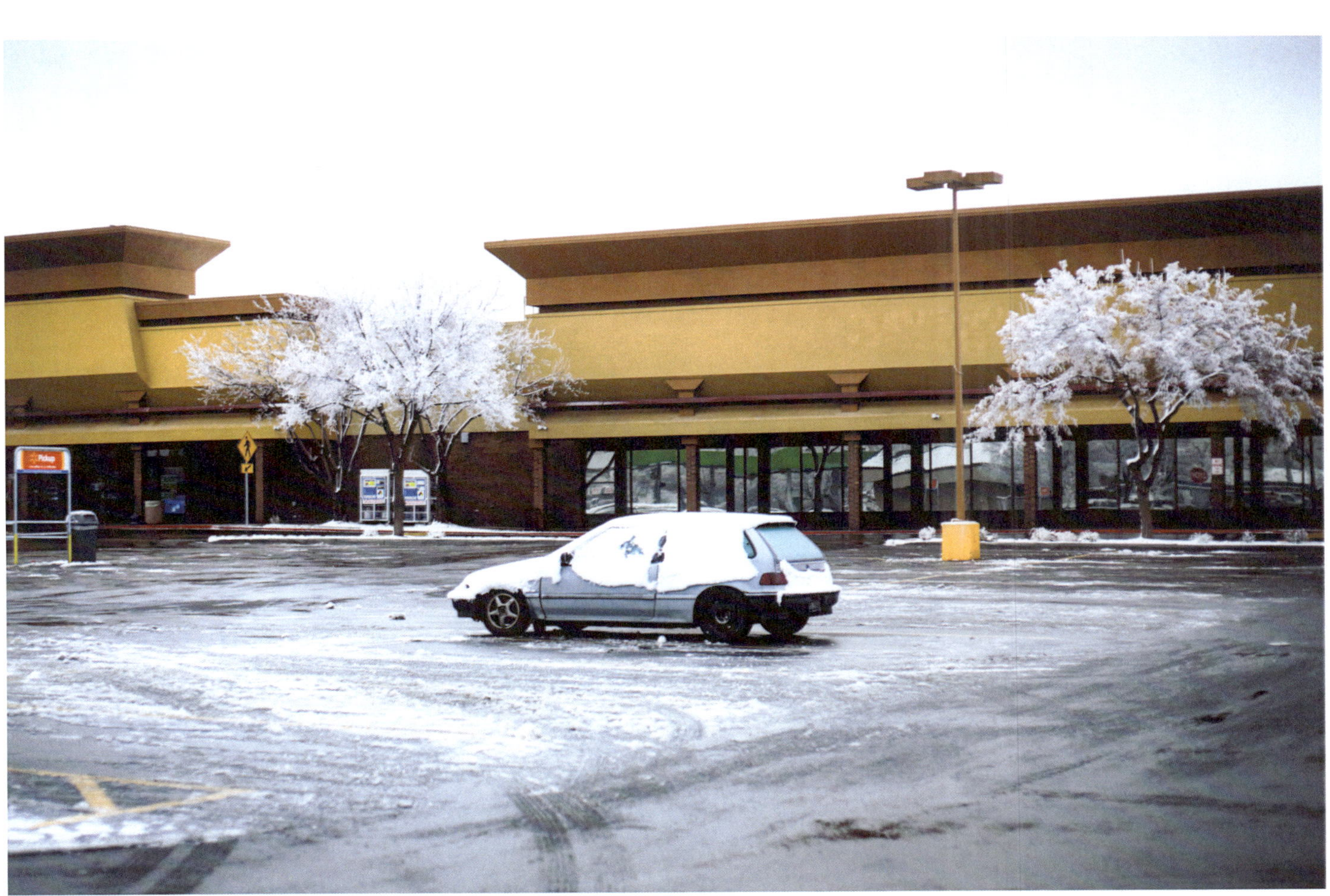

Pickup

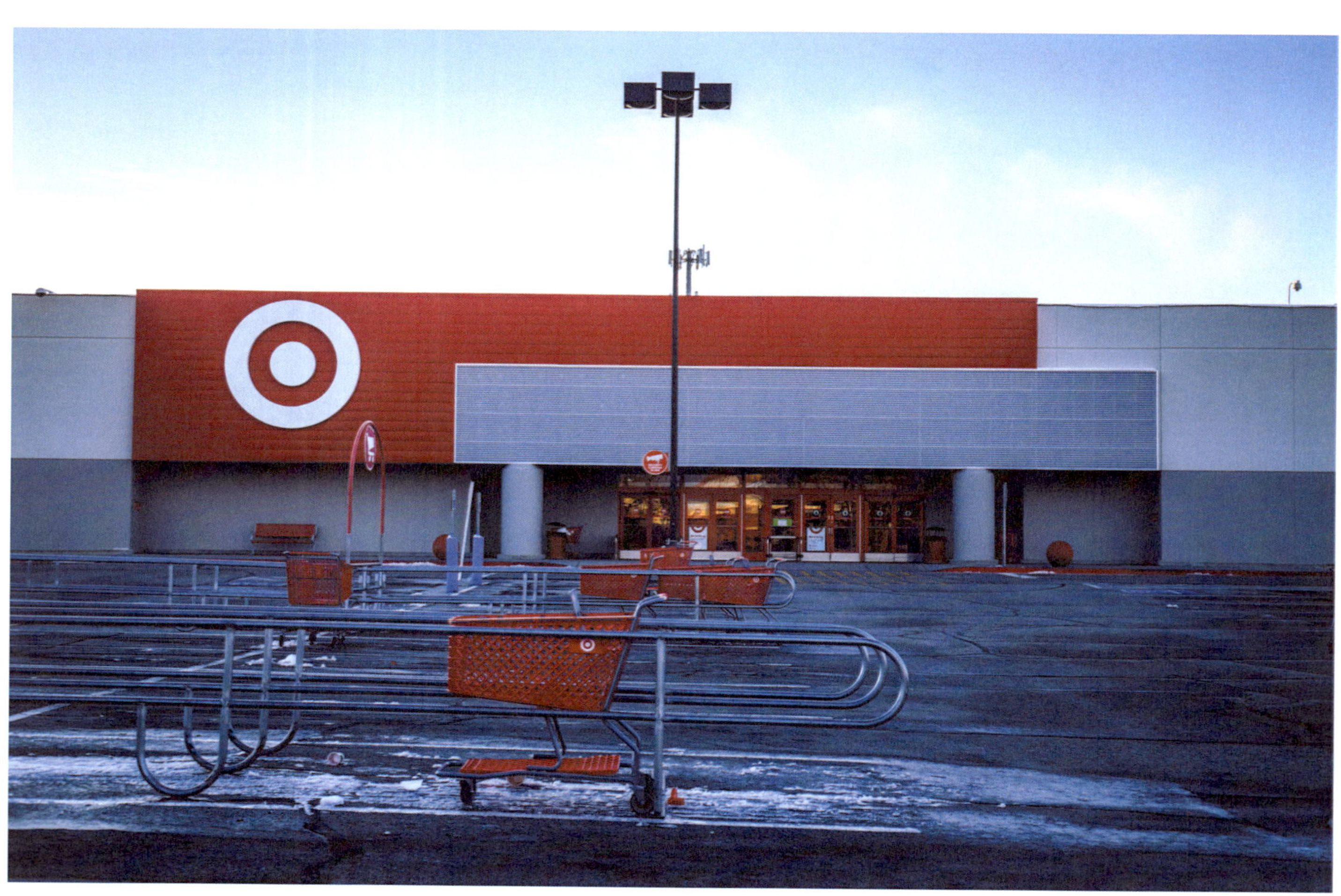

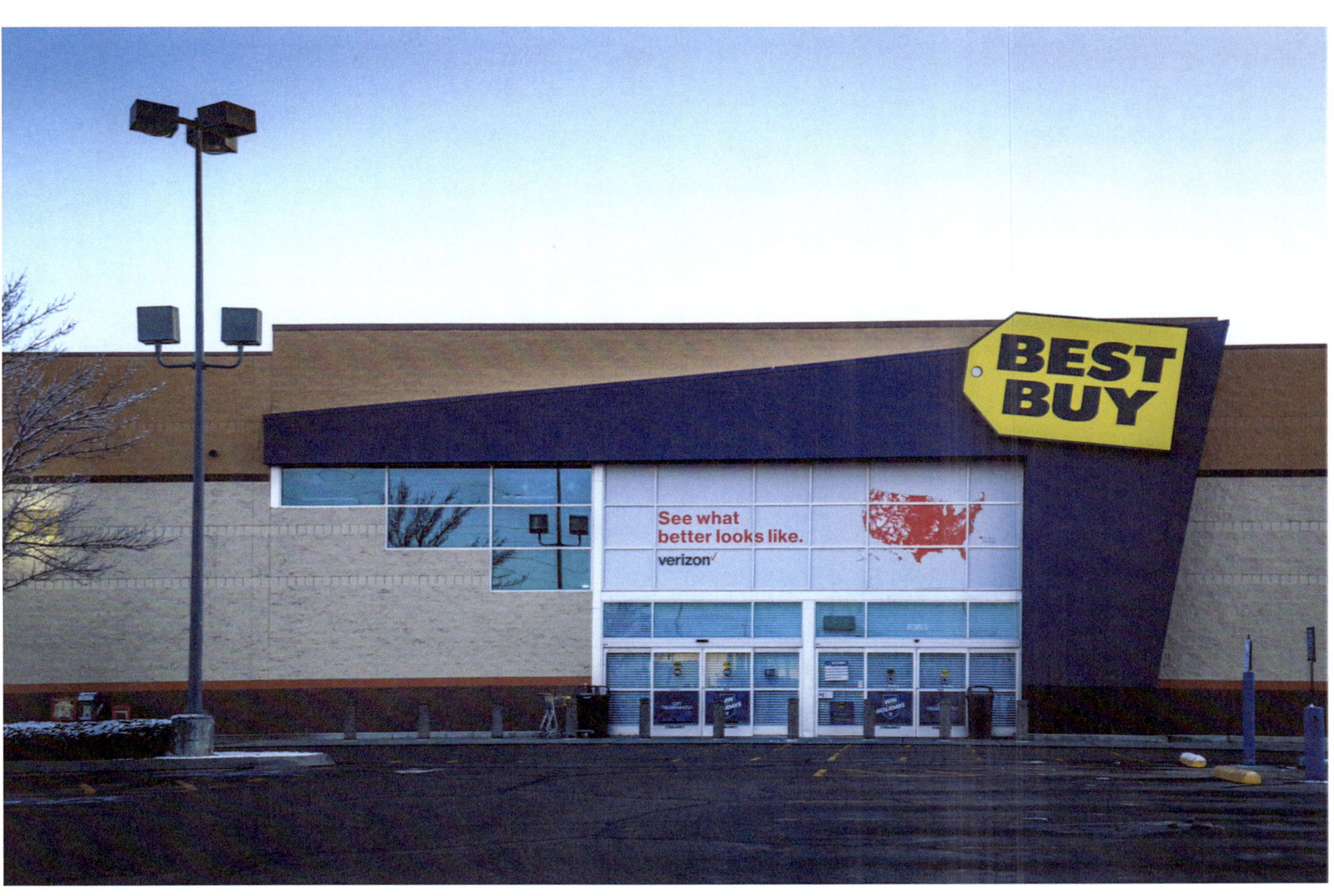

BEST
BUY
See what
better looks like.
verizon

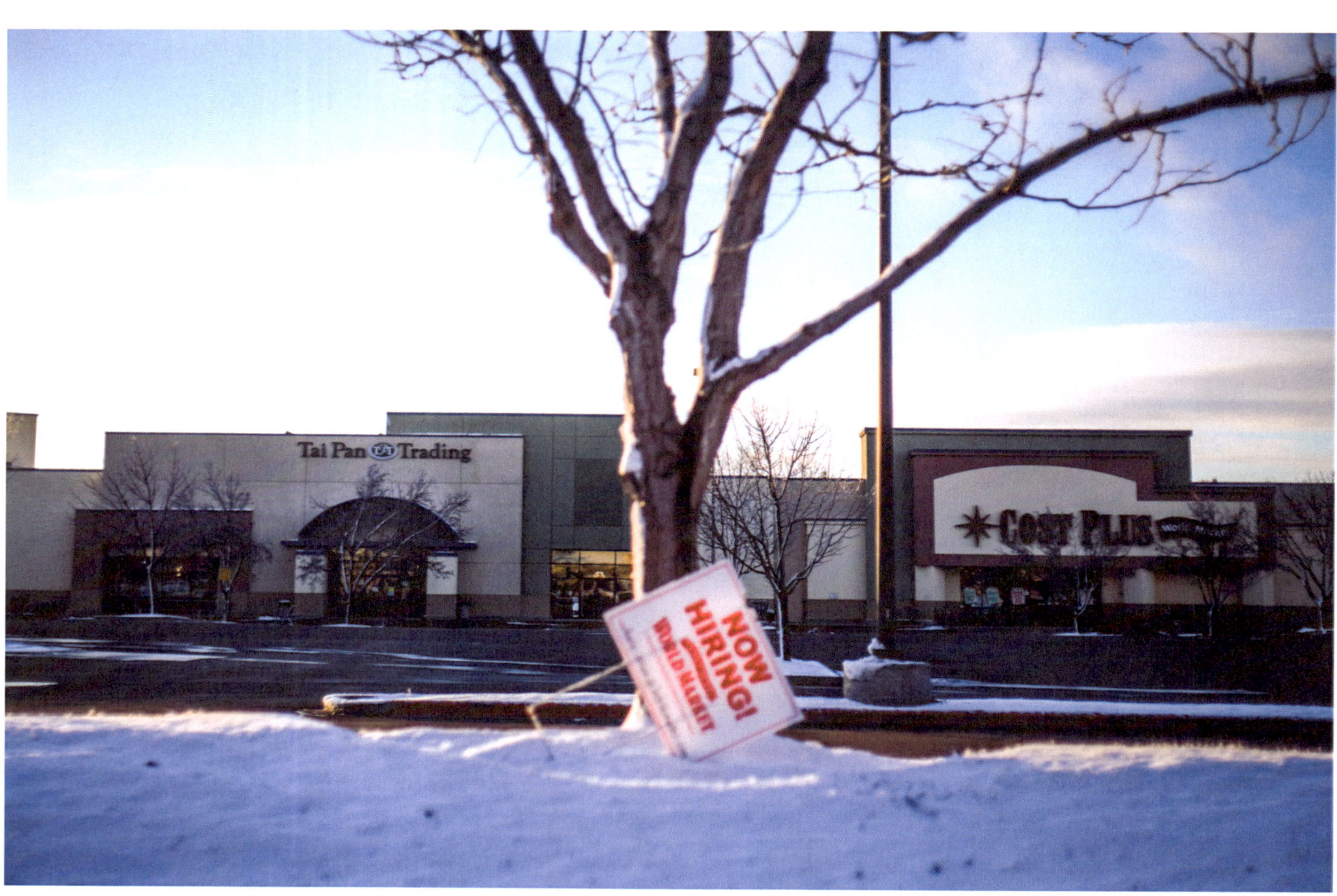

Tai Pan Trading
COST PLUS WORLD MARKET
NOW HIRING!
WORLD MARKET

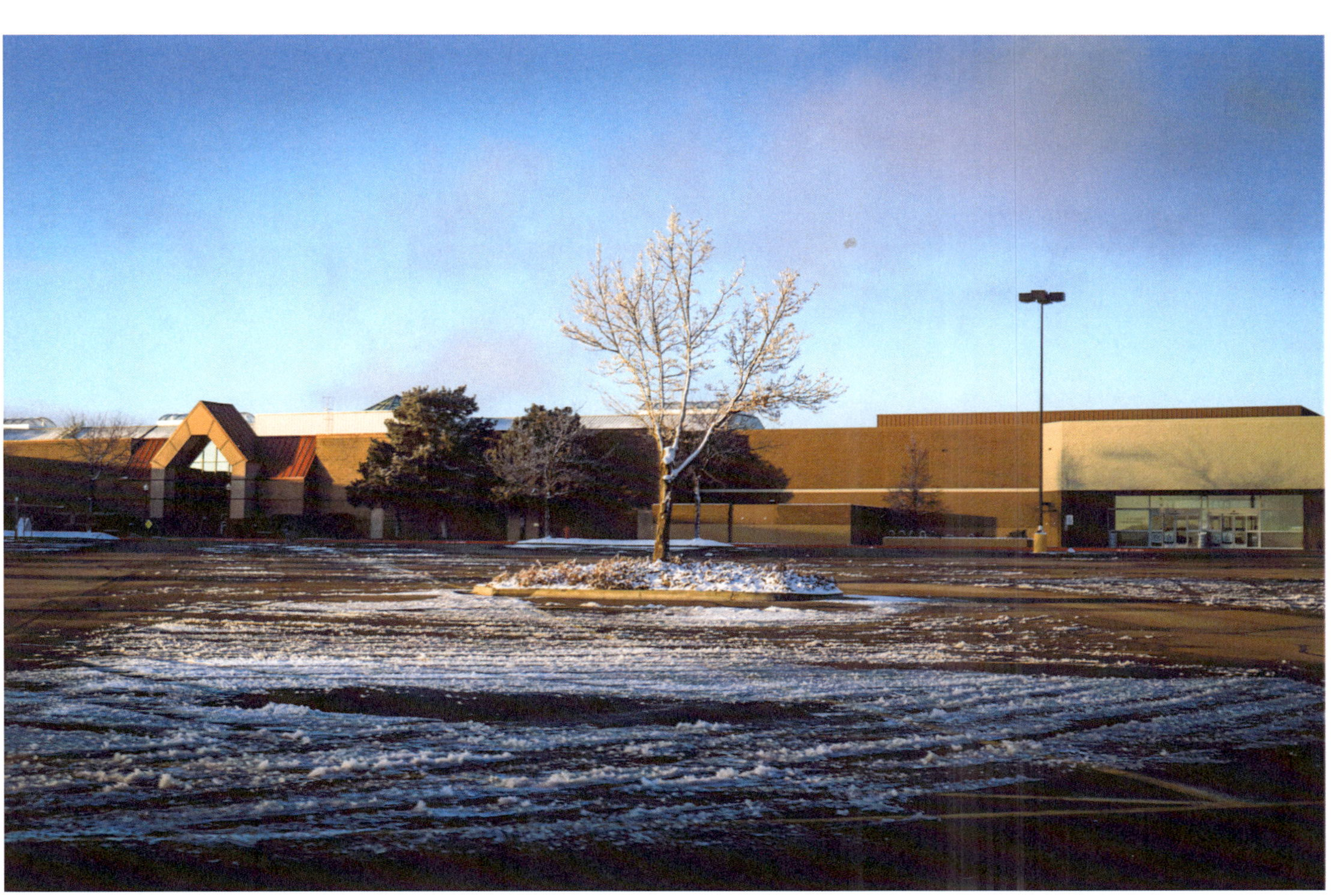

2 hours
56 minutes and
8 seconds
in downtown Los Angeles

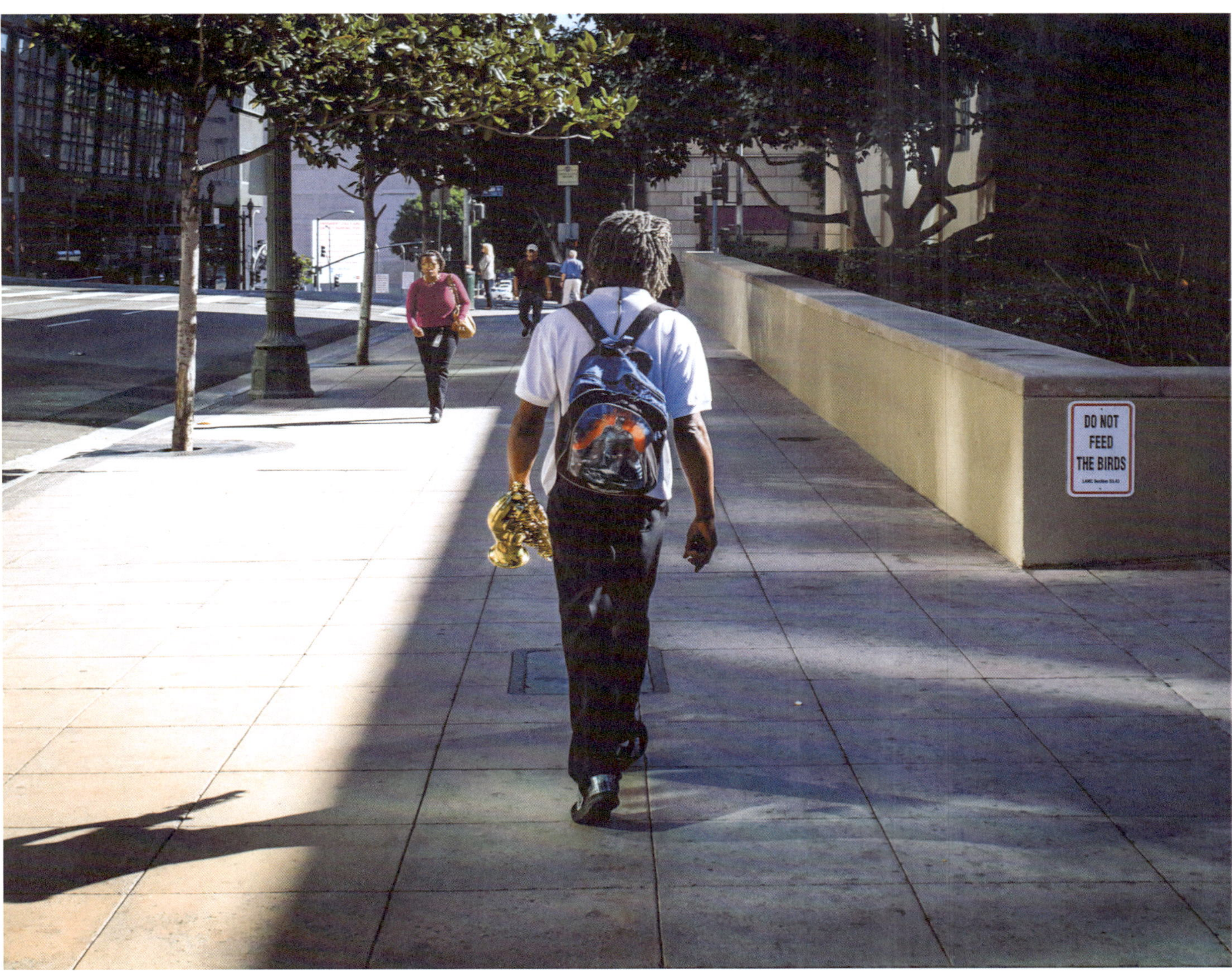

DO NOT
FEED
THE BIRDS
LAMC Section 53.42

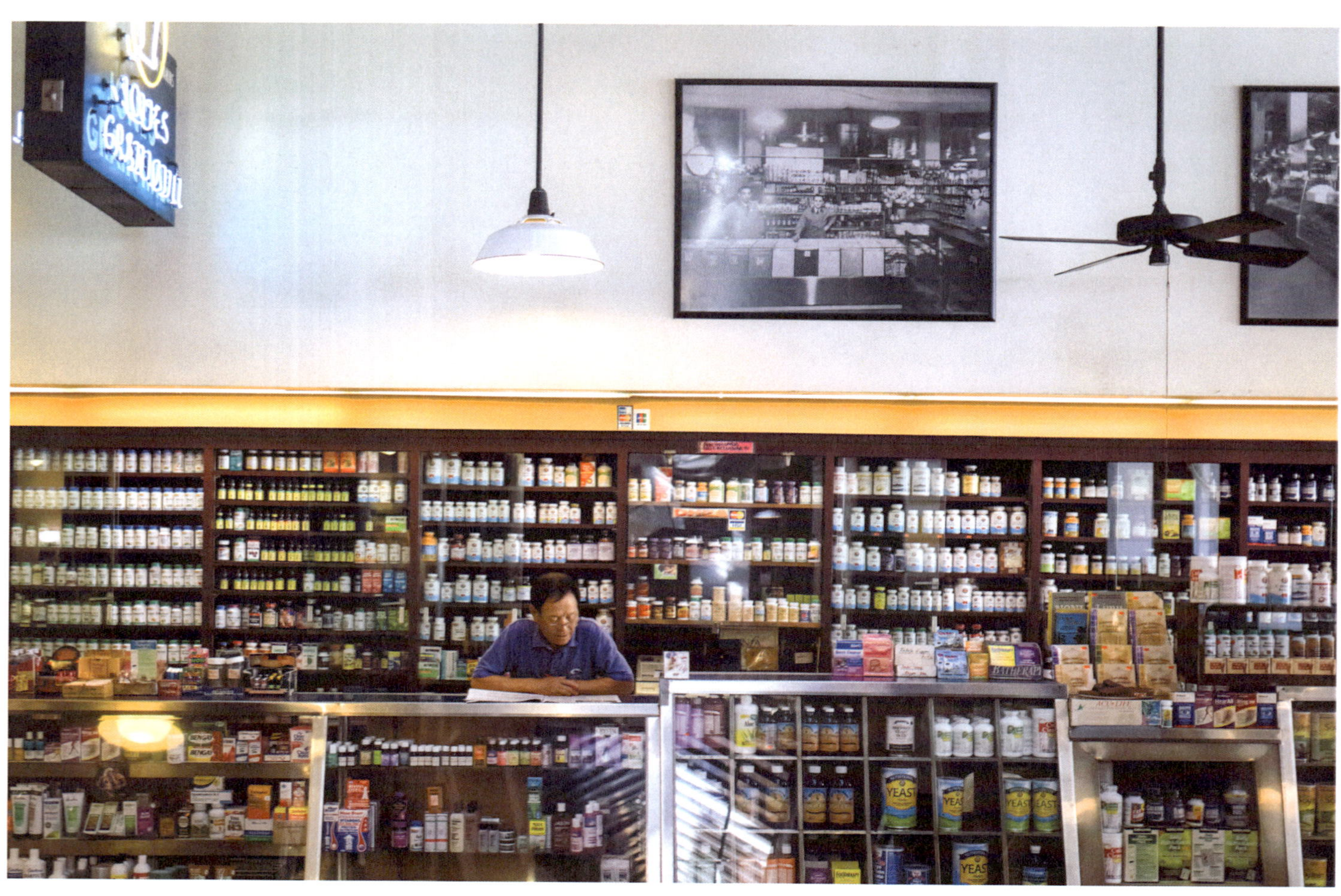

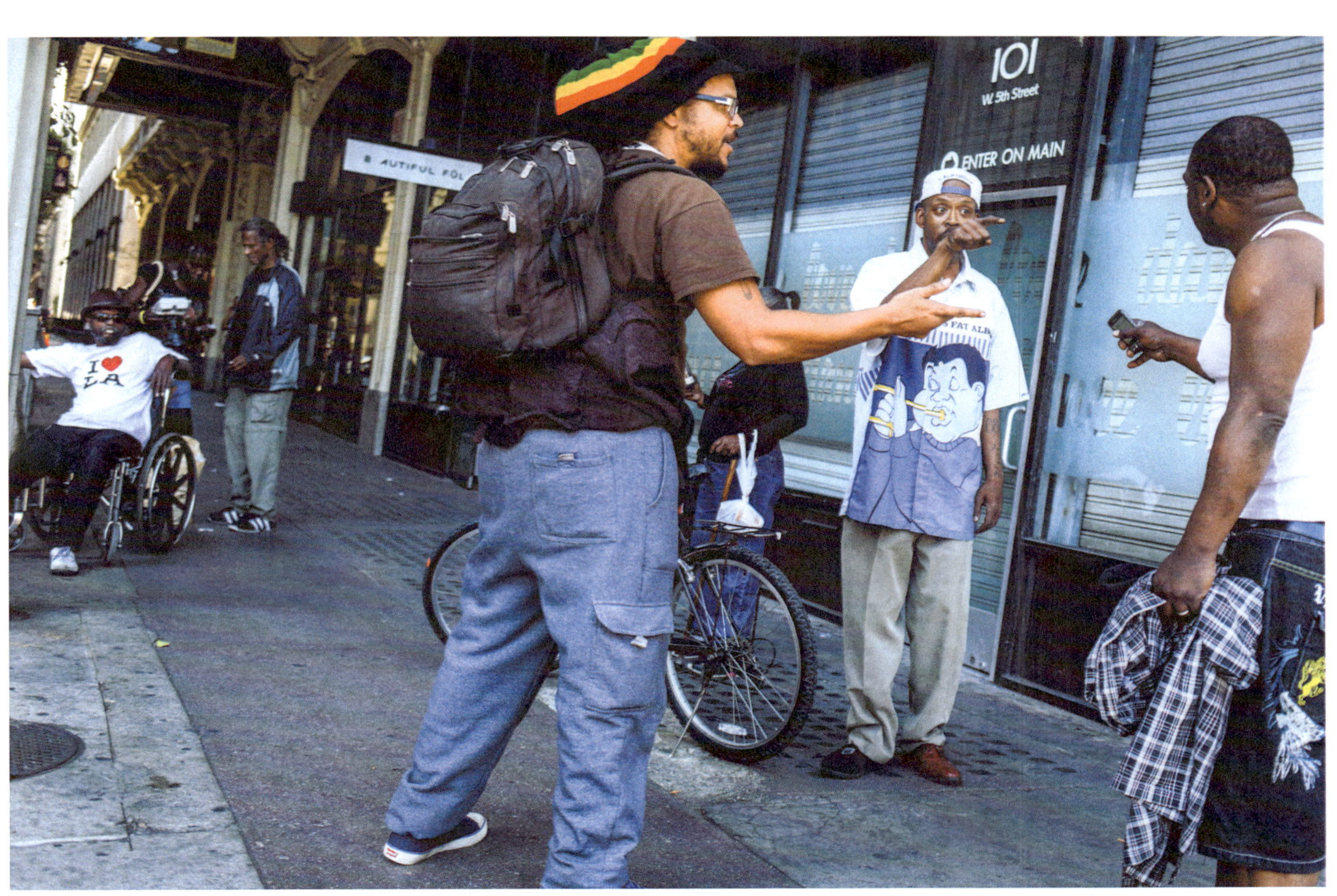
101
W. 5th Street
ENTER ON MAIN
I ♥ LA

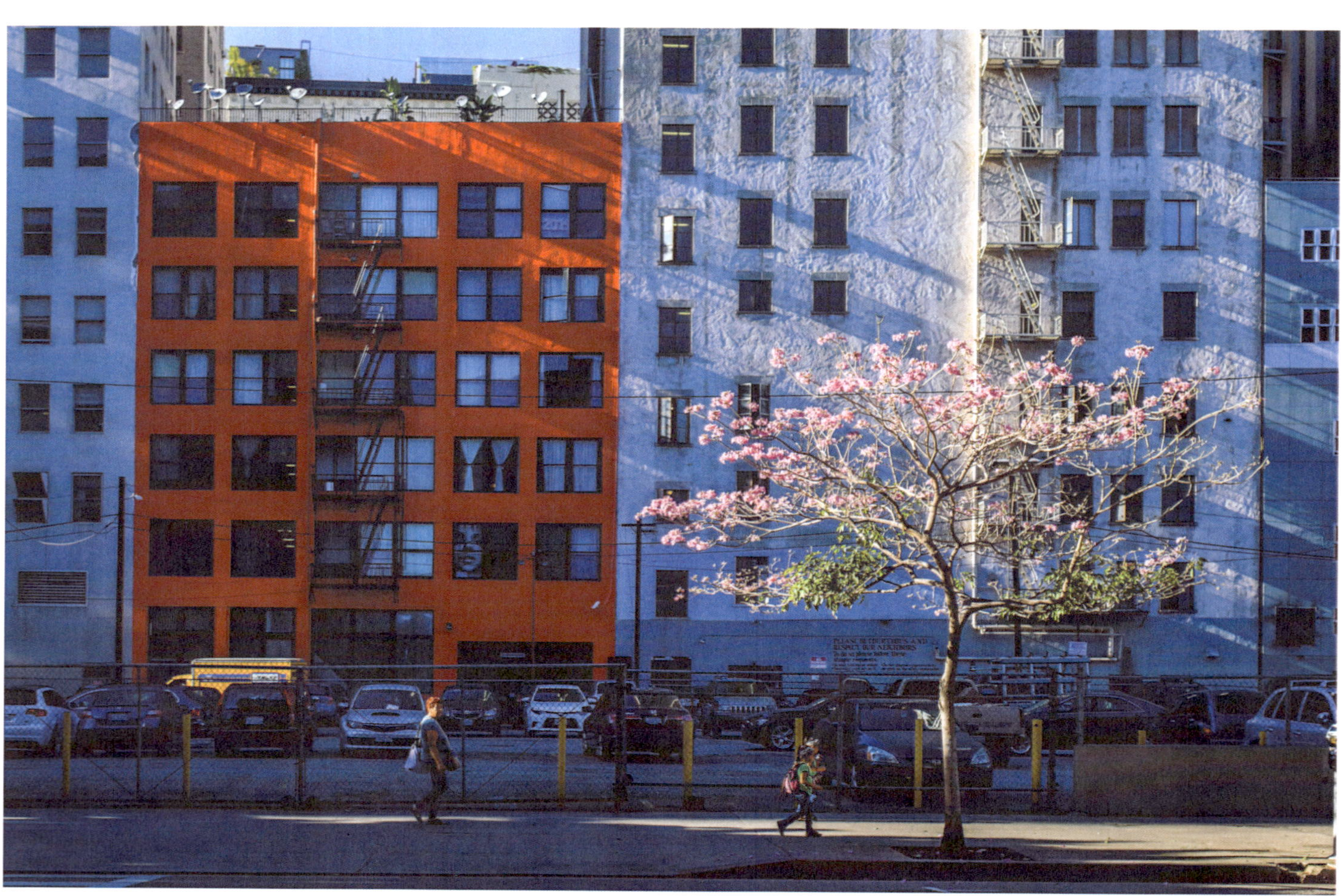

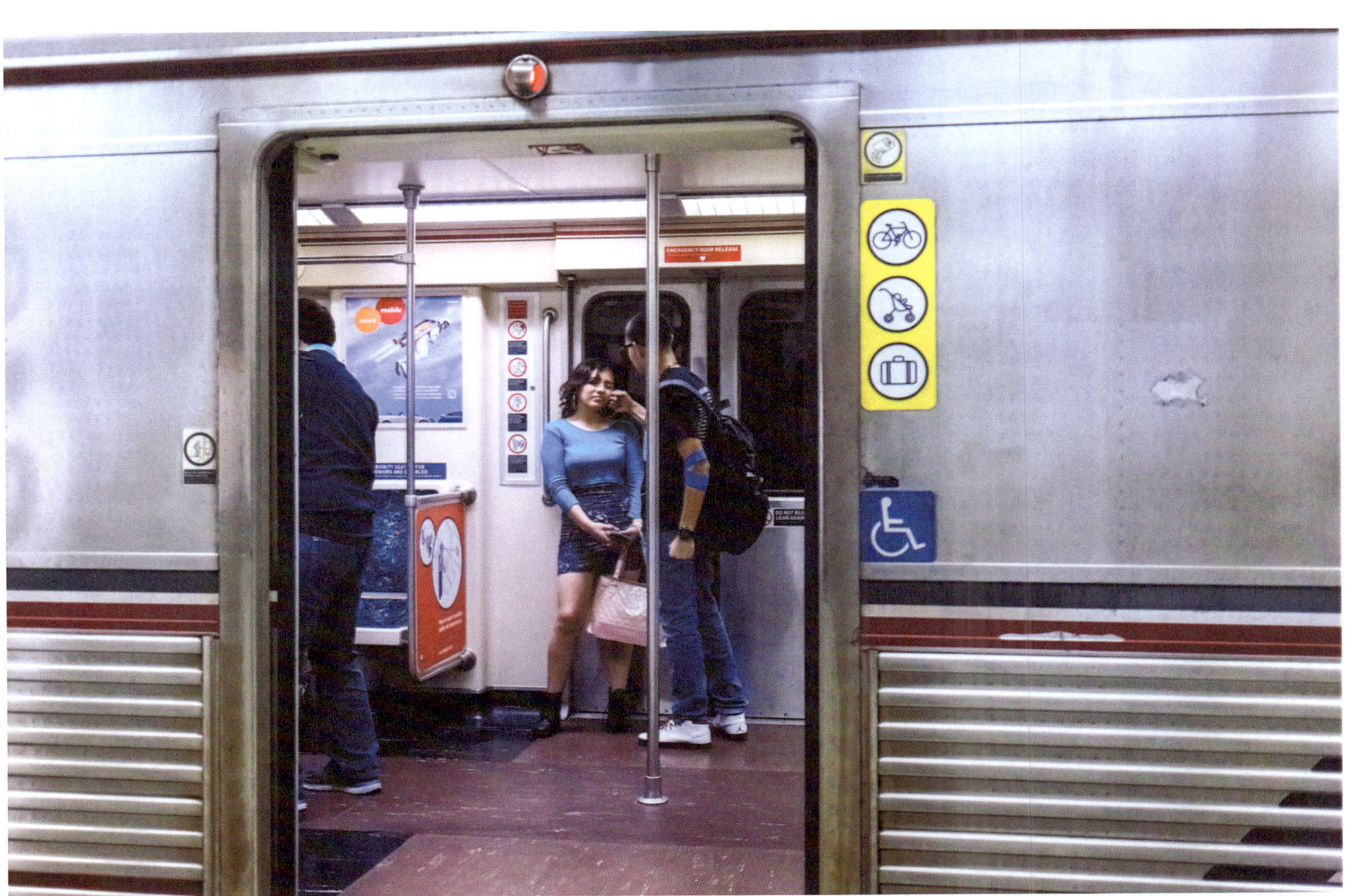

13 minutes and
10 seconds
sitting at approximately
34°01'21.6"N 118°30'52.5"W

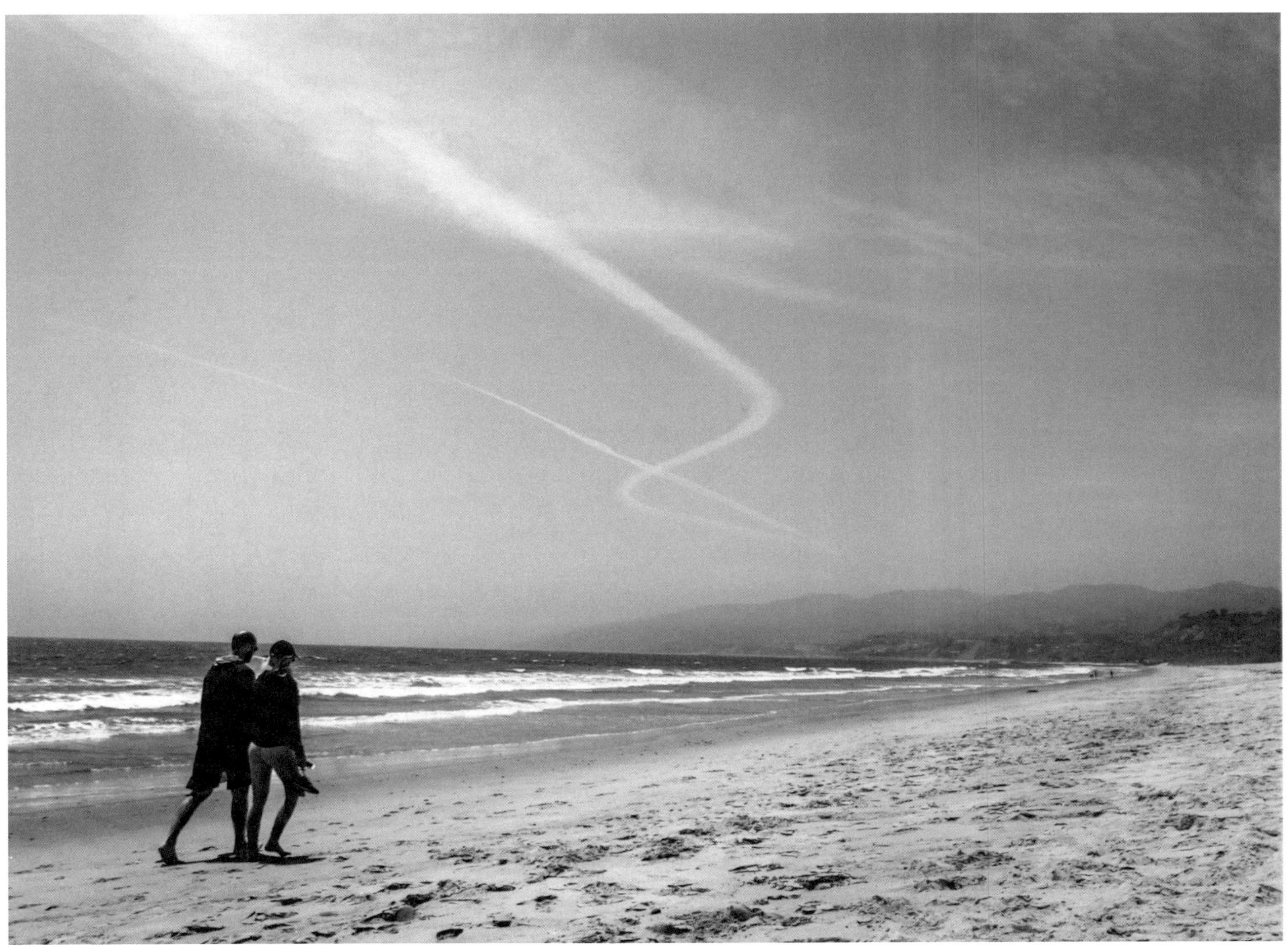

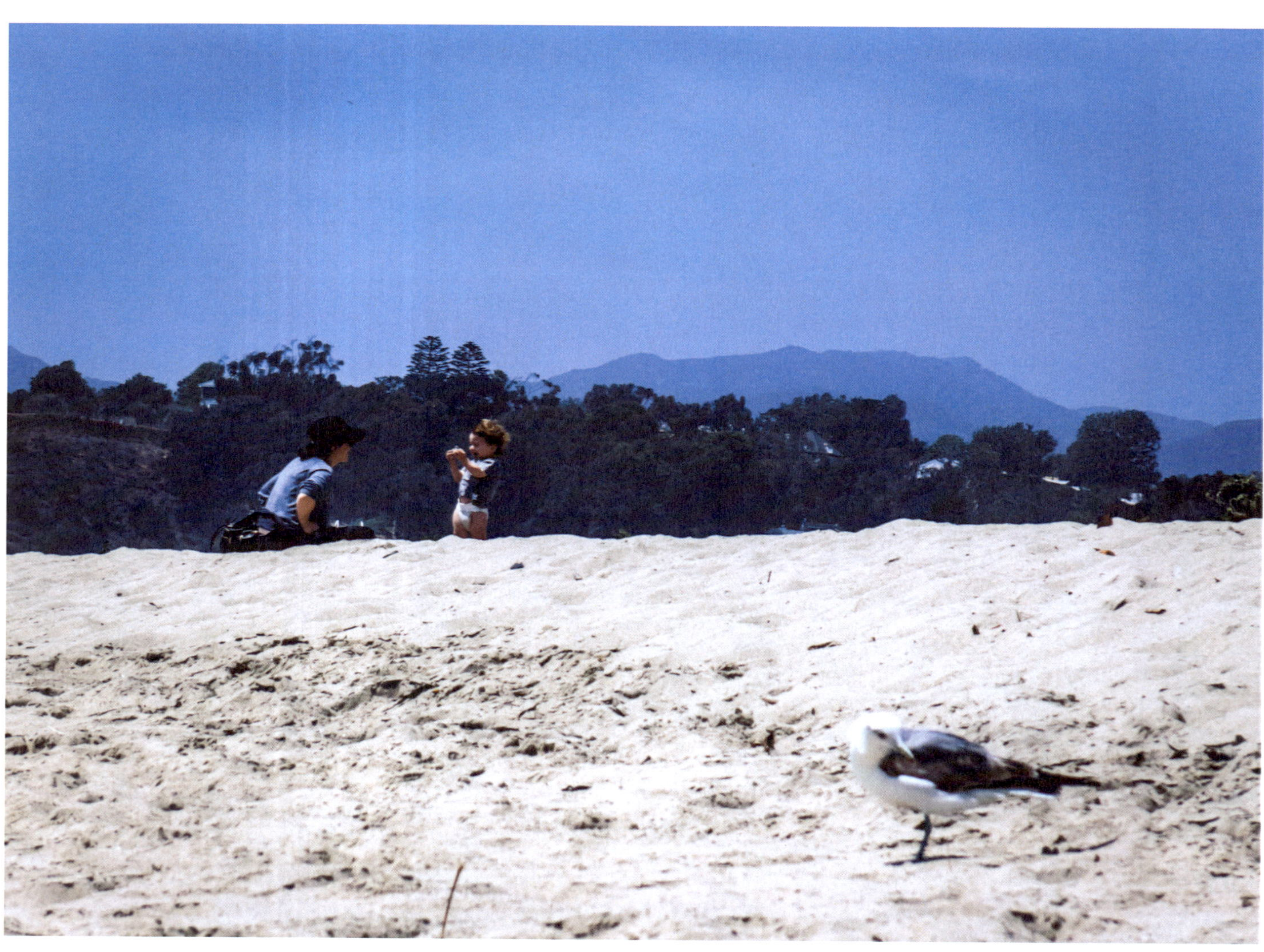

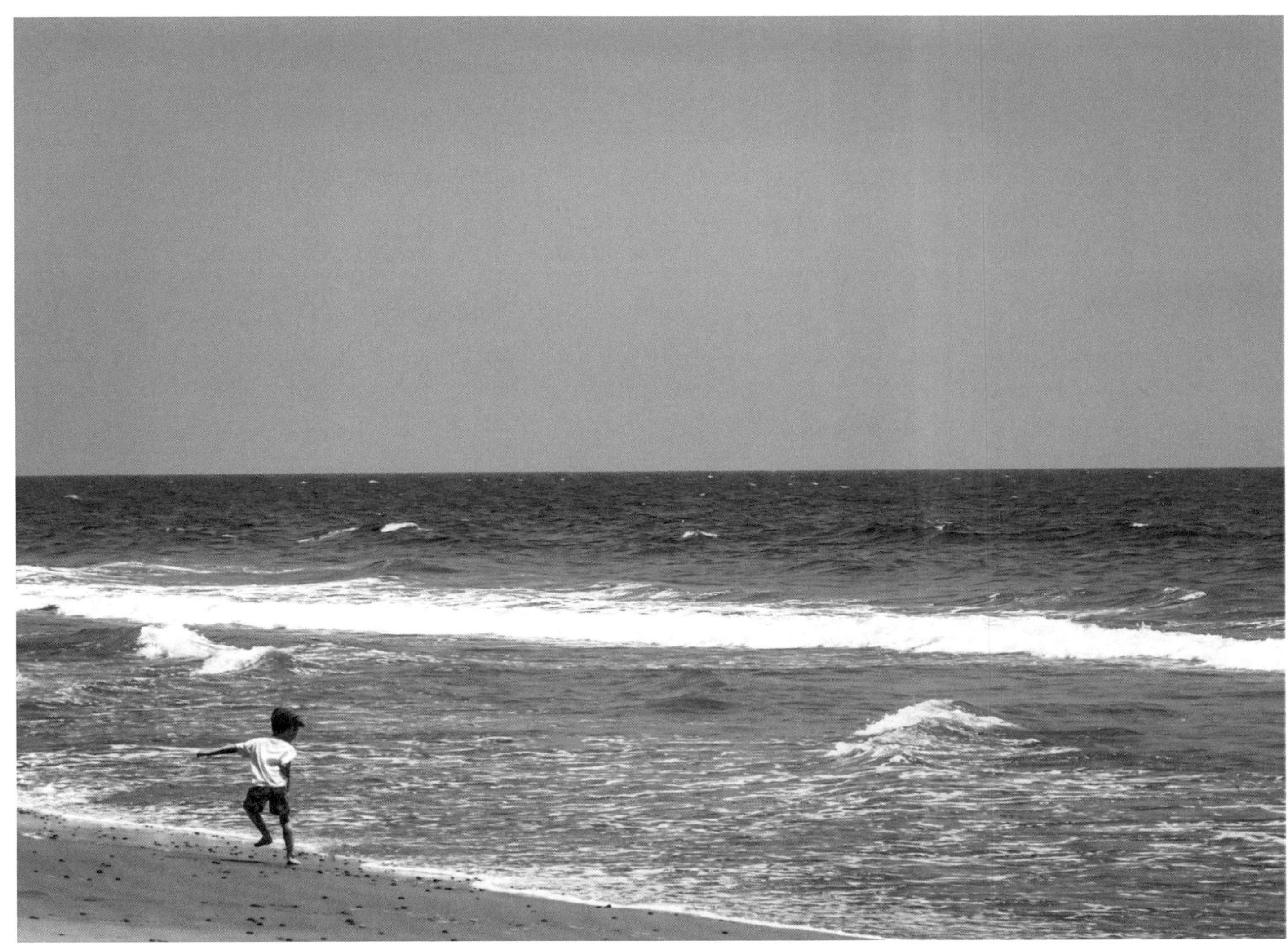

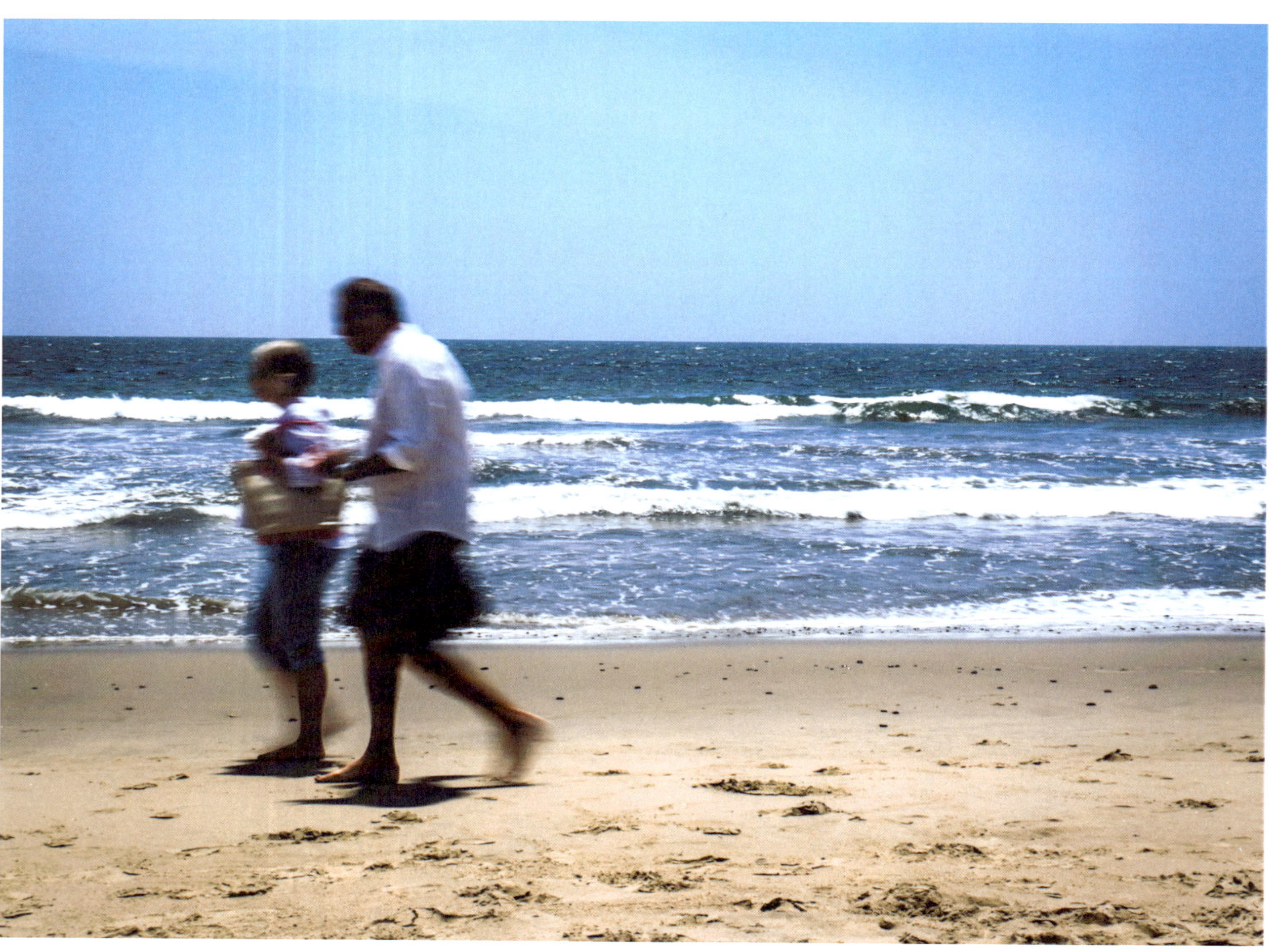

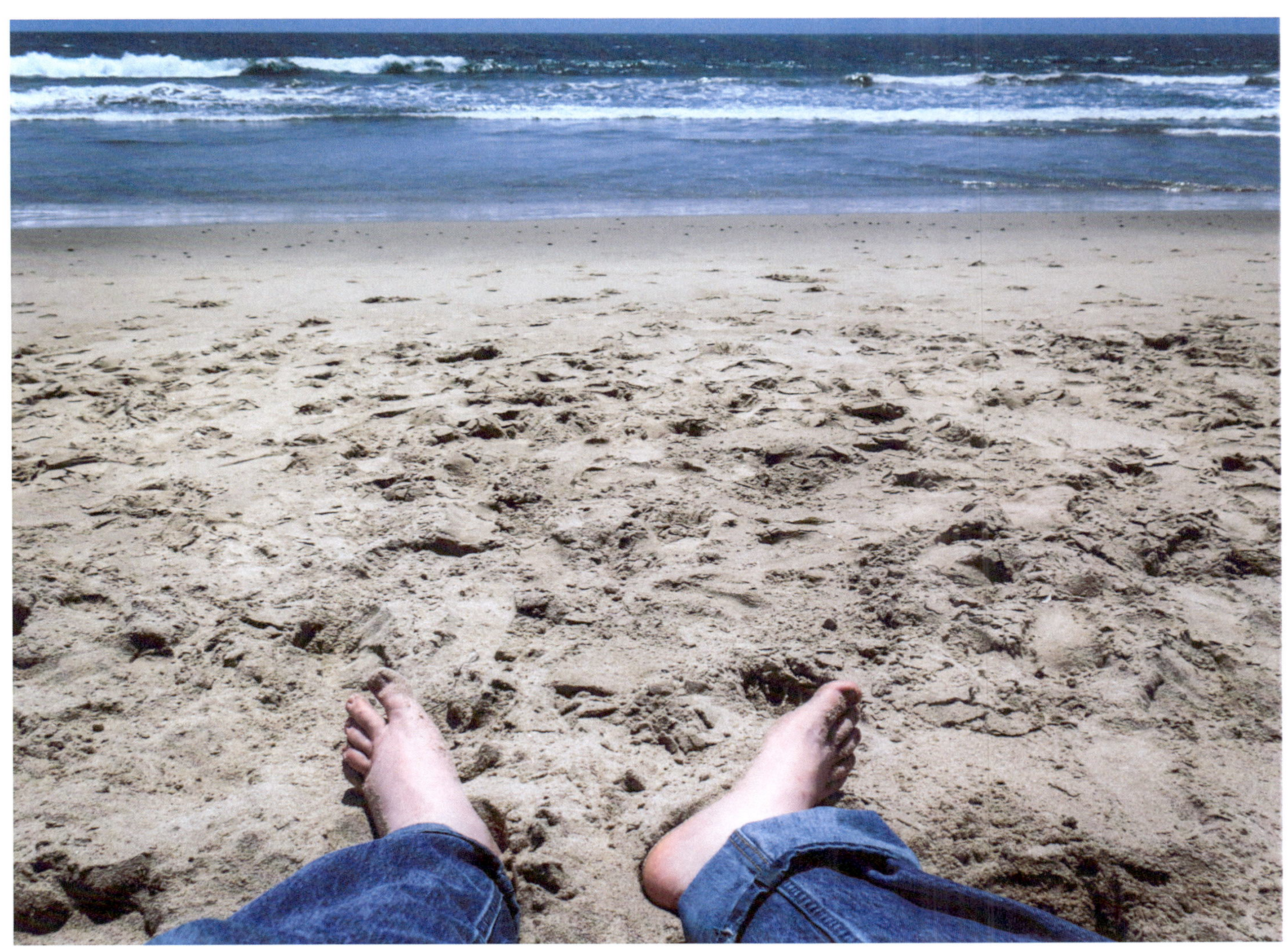

I should
probably replace
my baking sheets

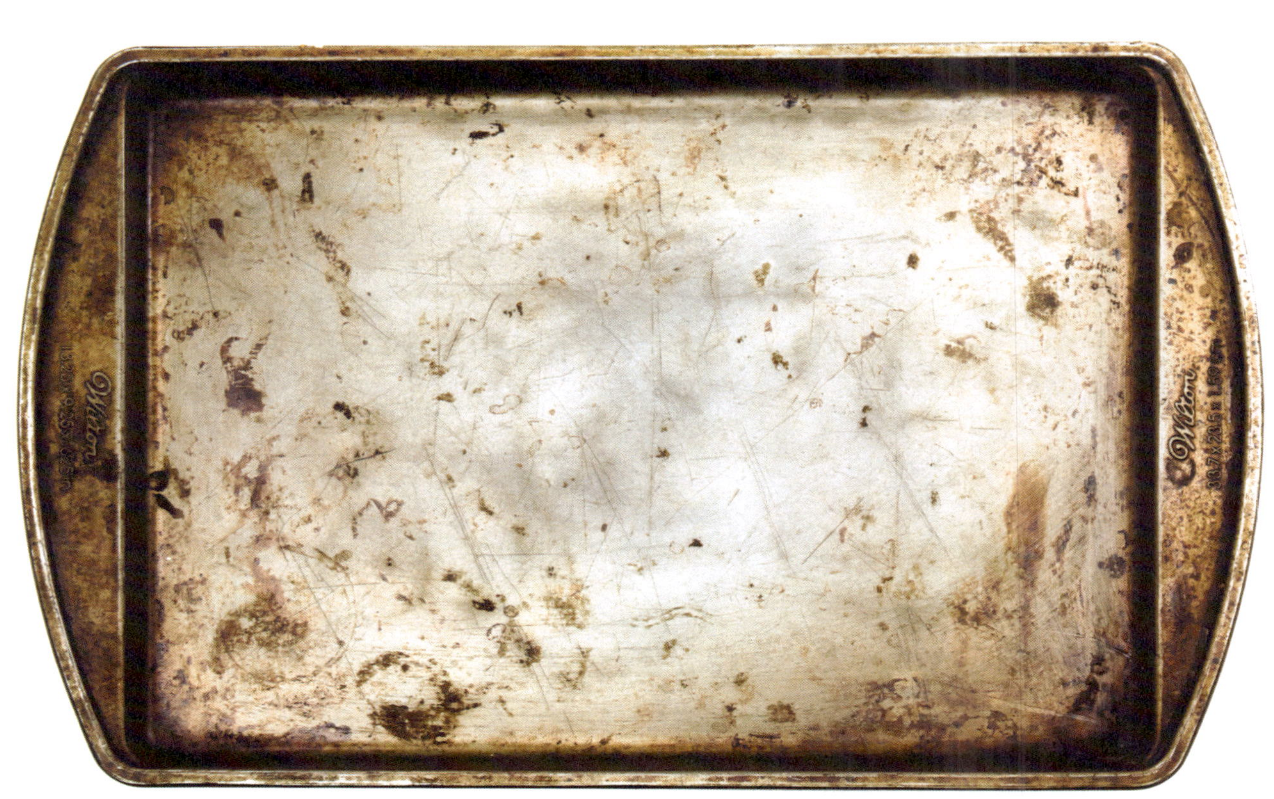

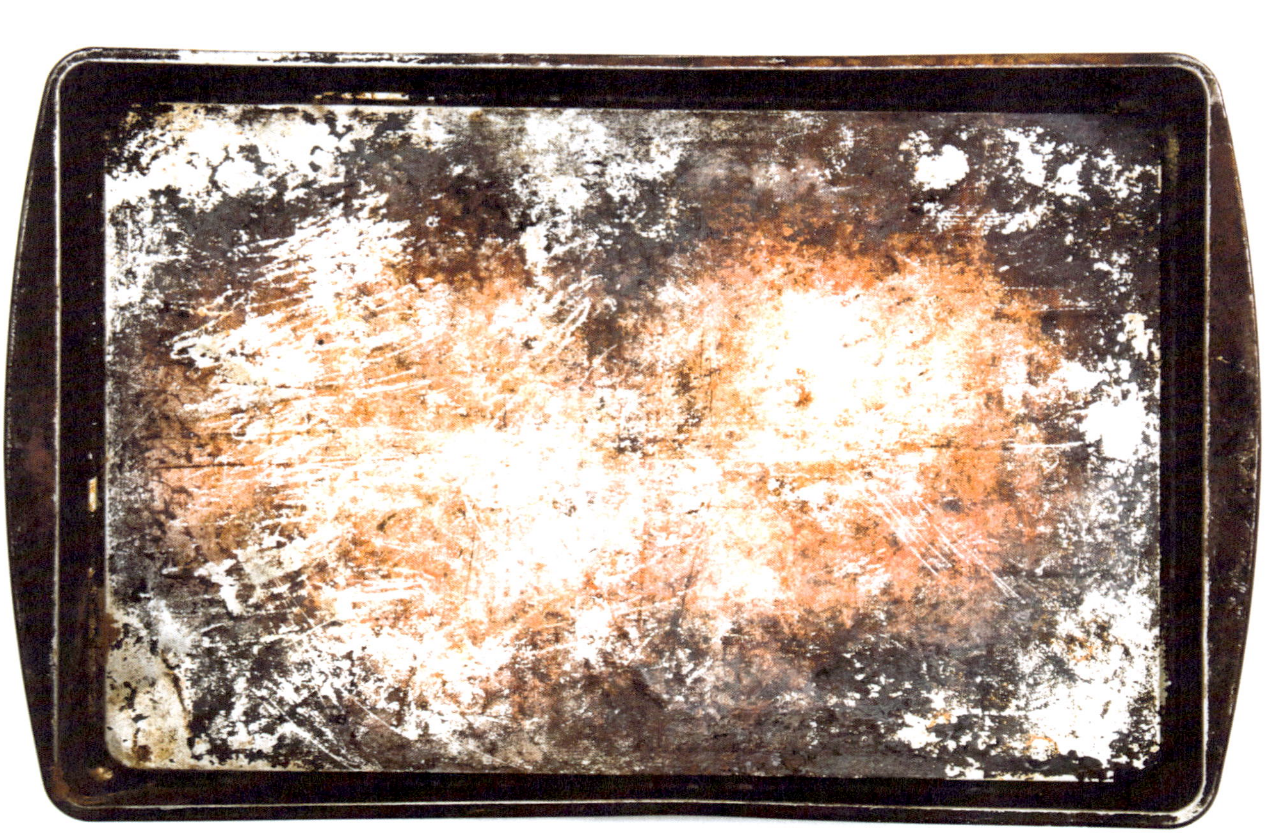

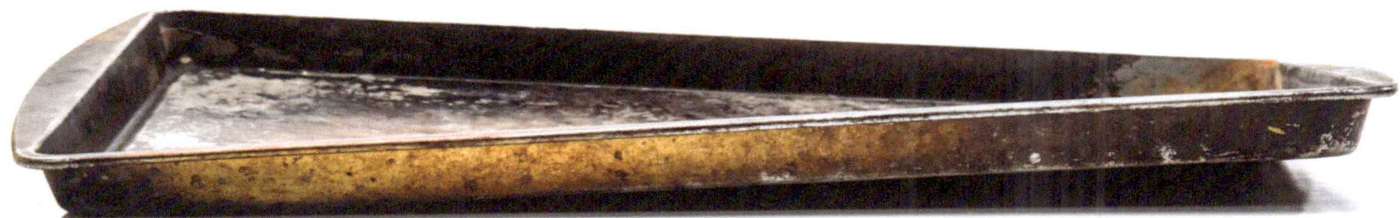

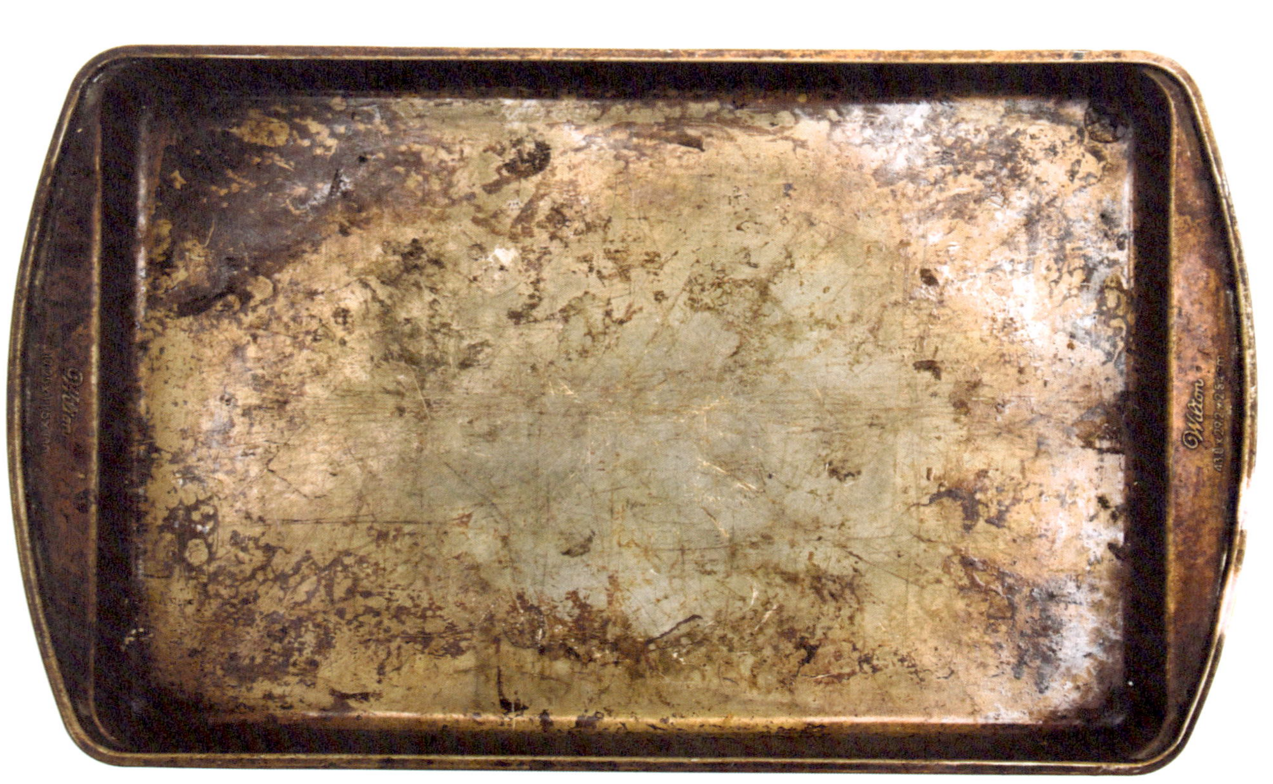

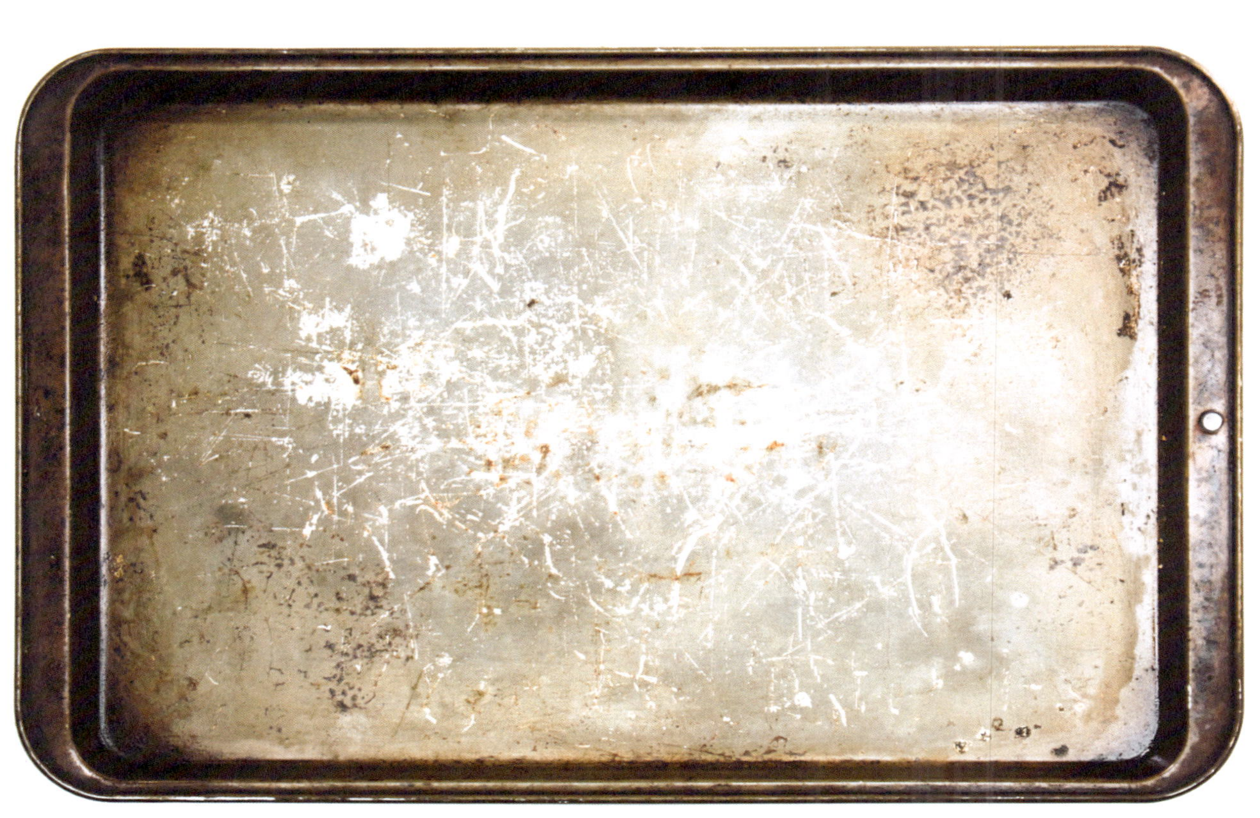